THE IDEA OF
NATURAL INEQUALITY
AND OTHER ESSAYS

THE IDEA OF
NATURAL INEQUALITY
AND OTHER ESSAYS

ANDRÉ BÉTEILLE
Delhi School of Economics

DELHI
OXFORD UNIVERSITY PRESS
BOMBAY CALCUTTA MADRAS
1983

Oxford University Press, Walton Street, Oxford OX2 6DP

LONDON GLASGOW NEW YORK TORONTO
DELHI BOMBAY CALCUTTA MADRAS KARACHI
KUALA LUMPUR SINGAPORE HONG KONG TOKYO
NAIROBI DAR ES SALAAM CAPE TOWN
MELBOURNE AUCKLAND

and associates in

BEIRUT BERLIN IBADAN MEXICO CITY NICOSIA

British Library Cataloguing in Publication Data
Beteille, Andre
The idea of natural inequality and other essays.
1. Equality
I. Title
305 HM146
ISBN 0-19-878004-4

Printed in India by P. K. Ghosh
at Eastend Printers, 3 Dr Suresh Sarkar Road, Calcutta 700014
and published by R. Dayal, Oxford University Press
2/11 Ansari Road, Daryaganj, New Delhi 110002

For Tara

Contents

Acknowledgements

The essays brought together in this volume were written on various occasions and delivered as lectures in places as far apart as Bombay, Cambridge, London and Sydney. I have in preparing and delivering the lectures received much kindness from people who are too numerous to be mentioned separately by name. I would like to thank those who invited me to deliver the lectures, and also those who sat and listened to them, if not appreciatively, at least patiently and courteously.

'The Idea of Natural Inequality' is reproduced by courtesy of The London School of Economics and Political Science which first published it as a pamphlet in 1980 and holds copyright in it; I am much obliged to Professor Ralf Dahrendorf for inviting me to deliver the thirteenth Auguste Comte Memorial Lecture of which it is the text. 'Homo Hierarchicus, Homo Equalis' is republished by courtesy of *Modern Asian Studies* where it was first published (vol. 13, no. 4) as the text of the Kingsley Martin Memorial Lecture delivered in March 1979; my warm thanks are due to Mr B. H. Farmer of St. John's College, Cambridge for making the occasion a memorable one for me and my wife. 'Harmonic and Disharmonic Social Systems' was first published in a different form but with the same title by Sydney University Press in 1971; I am greatly obliged to the Press for allowing me to republish it in this form and to Professor Marjorie Jacobs for her generous hospitality in Sydney in the summer—their winter—of 1971. 'The Backward Classes and the New Social Order' was earlier published as a separate pamphlet by Oxford University Press in 1981; it is based on the B. R. Ambedkar Memorial Lectures delivered in Bombay on 6 and 7 March 1980, and I would like to thank the University of Bombay for inviting me to deliver them. 'The Pursuit of Equality and the Indian University' is a revised version of the Duhr Memorial Lecture delivered in St Xavier's College, Bombay in November 1980 and published in another form and under the title 'The Indian University: Academic Standards and the Pursuit

of Equality' in *Minerva*, vol. 19, no. 2 (Summer 1981); I am grateful
to Fr. John Correia-Alfonso S.J., Principal, St Xavier's College,
Bombay for inviting me to deliver the lecture and to Professor
Edward Shils for publishing the essay in *Minerva* and permitting me
to republish it here. 'Equality of Opportunity' was delivered as the
G. L. Mehta Memorial Lecture in March 1982 at the Indian Institute of Technology, Bombay which I would like to thank for the
invitation; I would also like to acknowledge my debt to the late
Mr Mehta's family for their kindness to me in Bombay.

Mr Vinay Srivastava, Lecturer in Sociology, Hindu College has
once again put me in his debt by preparing the Index.

31 December 1982   André Béteille

Introduction

I have brought together in this collection a number of essays dealing with various aspects of inequality with special reference to contemporary India, but viewed in a comparative perspective. They were all delivered as lectures, some in India and some outside. All the lectures were delivered between March 1979 and March 1982, except one, 'Harmonic and Disharmonic Social Systems', which was delivered in July 1971. However, this has been almost completely rewritten for the present volume while keeping within the broad framework of the original lecture.

Although the essays were all written as lectures, they were written also for publication. All of them have in fact been previously published, either as separate pamphlets or in periodicals. One was serialized by two daily papers, without my knowledge and initially to my embarrassment. I have tried in each essay to address a general but informed audience without sacrificing too much the weight and rigour that I consider to be essential to the practice of an academic discipline.

A lecture, however carefully or diligently written, is different from a paper prepared for publication in a professional journal. It has a different purpose. Professional journals are now rarely read outside the profession; most of them have become so specialized that they can be read with profit by only those who work in a particular discipline or in a particular branch of it. When scholars write in such journals, they write mainly for each other, and it is mainly through these publications that technical advances are now made in a scholarly discipline. But scholars have also an obligation to present the results of their work to larger audiences. The memorial lecture, organized by a university or a college, is an ideal occasion for this kind of presentation. Most of the essays printed here were memorial lectures, and they were all delivered in institutions of higher learning.

These essays are part of an effort to develop a language in which the sociologist can address not only his fellow sociologists, but also other social scientists as well as the general reader. By its nature, this has to be a continuing effort. Each academic discipline develops its own specialized terminology as a necessary part of the rigorous pursuit of particular problems of enquiry and analysis. But the language of discourse in the science of man and society cannot acquire a life of its own; it has to depend for nourishment on the language of everyday life.

I have in these essays not only addressed myself to general questions but also drawn my arguments and examples from a variety of disciplines. My own professional interest in the subject of inequality derives from my work as a sociologist, but I have not felt constrained in these essays to confine myself to strictly sociological ground. It would be difficult to exaggerate the contributions made by the discipline of sociology to the illumination of inequality in areas such as occupational ranking or social mobility. While fully appreciating these contributions, I have addressed myself to problems that are of common interest to the social or the human sciences rather than to those with which only the sociologist is mainly concerned.

Apart from sociology, the disciplines across which I have ranged include history, philosophy and law. A central concern in all the essays is with changes in patterns of inequality: in the distribution of things, in the relations between persons, and in legal and moral conceptions. It is impossible, without some attention to the historical record, to determine which aspects of inequality in our contemporary life are lasting and durable, and which ones are fleeting and transient. The fact that I lack the expert's mastery of historical material has not deterred me from drawing upon this material to illustrate my arguments. But I have used the material in the spirit of a sociologist: not so much to reconstruct the past as to illuminate the present. I cannot emphasize too strongly that my concern has been with the present which I consider to be the sociologist's main concern.

I have allowed myself to enter more directly and more openly into normative questions than is commonly done by sociologists, although here practice has varied greatly among them. Sociologists are far less confident today than they were a generation ago about the ease with which facts can be separated from values and about their capacity for constructing a value-free science of society. Most of the essays in this collection deal with questions of value in one form or another. In discussing alternative measures for the attainment of equality, I have on occasion given my own judgement, although I have tried in each case to make the grounds for my judgement sufficiently clear.

It has been an established part of scholarly convention to distinguish between the natural and the moral sciences. Sociology has occupied an uneasy position between the two, and no doubt these essays illustrate the ambiguities inherent in that position. To acknowledge the central place of values in social and human affairs is not to deny the need to be attentive to facts. Public debate on inequality, particularly in India, suffers too often from insufficient attention to empirical evidence. This evidence is by its nature highly diverse, and I have in these essays had occasion to refer to material ranging from university and college enrolments to Supreme Court judgements.

I would not claim for the volume greater unity than one would expect in a collection of essays on a common theme but written for various occasions. It may be said that the essays represent not so much a single point of view as the point of view of a single person confronted with successive dilemmas. There are shifts in emphasis as well as in the ground from which the same order of reality is viewed. The essays seek to combine social criticism with social analysis, but the critical approach is directed at one and the same time to two alternative, even competing, types of social formation: the traditional hierarchical order and the modern system of inequality generated by the market and the state.

I would like to draw attention to these dilemmas which are a source of ambiguity in much social criticism, and, at a certain remove, in much social analysis in contemporary India. The Indian social scientist lives at much closer quarters than his Western counterpart with a traditional social order towards which his attitude cannot but be ambivalent. Much of his criticism of this social order is made in terms of the concepts and categories of the modern world. But these concepts and categories, and the modern world in which they have their place are not immune to criticism despite their privileged status. Caught in this dilemma, the Indian social scientist finds it difficult to achieve a balance between his disaffection with the past and his doubts about the present; and the balance he achieves for one occasion need not be the same for all occasions.

In 'The Idea of Natural Inequality' which was my Auguste Comte Memorial Lecture, I ask whether the justification of inequality in fact disappears with the establishment of modern democracies. It is a critique of what may be called the 'scientific theory of inequality' which is characteristic of modern capitalism and, more generally, of all modern societies. 'Possessive individualism' generates its own structure of inequalities, and modern societies explain and also justify these inequalities by means of elaborate and complex theories. I have sought to invite comparison between these scientific theories of the 'inequality of men' and traditional theories, rooted in religion, explaining and justifying social hierarchy.

'Homo Hierarchicus, Homo Equalis', which was the Kingsley Martin Memorial Lecture for 1979, examines the presuppositions behind the contrast, frequently made, between India and the West. In this contrast, which I subject to critical examination, India is viewed as the exemplar of hierarchy and the West as the exemplar of equality. My argument in the essay is that no major civilization has ever fully excluded a concern for equality, and that inequality—not only the fact of inequality but the need to explain and justify it—bedevils every modern society. I draw attention to the paradox that Western societies were acquiring a new and comprehensive commitment to equality at precisely that juncture in their history when they were also developing in their fullest form the theory and practice of imperialism.

For all this, we cannot ignore the uniqueness of the modern world. It no longer incorporates a general, a comprehensive scheme of hierarchy accepted or at least acknowledged by most if not all members of society. I examine this contrast between traditional and modern societies in the essay entitled 'Harmonic and Disharmonic Social Systems' which is based on a lecture delivered in the University of Sydney in 1971. Harmonic systems are those in which there is a general acceptance of the social hierarchy as corresponding to the natural scheme of things; in pre-modern times—and, indeed, well into early modern times—the hierarchical conception of society prevailed in Europe as well as in India. By contrast, contemporary societies are permeated by the contradiction between the fact of inequality and the ideal of equality and in that sense constitute disharmonic systems.

The commitment to equality is now very marked in all modern societies, not least in those which were rigidly hierarchical in the

past. This commitment has to contend with material constraints that
vary greatly from one society to another. A close look at the commitment to equality shows how complex the idea of equality is. It
is not a simple or a unitary concept, but is made up of components
that are diverse and difficult to reconcile. In the two Ambedkar
Memorial Lectures entitled 'The Backward Classes and the New
Social Order' I examine some of the problems of reconciling the
divergent conceptions of equality and of making the ideal of equality
real under conditions of scarcity.

In these two lectures I attempt a sociological critique of the
equality provisions in the Constitution of India of which Dr Ambedkar was a principal architect. In doing so I intrude extensively and
perhaps unwisely into the terrain of legal studies. I have not tried to
examine all aspects of the Constitution, confining myself mainly to
those which directly affect the weaker sections of Indian society, in
particular the Scheduled Castes and the Scheduled Tribes. I consider
in some detail the tension between the meritarian principle and the
compensatory principle (or the principle of redress) in the light of
the Constitutional commitment to creating equality of status and of
opportunity.

'The Pursuit of Equality and the Indian University' is based on
the Duhr Memorial Lecture delivered at St. Xavier's College,
Bombay in November 1980. In it I examine the relationship between
university education and social mobility in a comparative and
historical perspective. It tends to be forgotten that until about a
hundred years ago the universities in the West were themselves
hierarchical institutions, exclusively male and attentive to social
distinctions. Indian universities are changing their orientation towards equality and social mobility. They are open to men and women
without distinction of class, caste or creed. But by their very nature
universities have to make their own distinctions according to academic achievement and merit. The basic question is how far these
reproduce the old distinctions of caste, class and gender embedded
in the environment within which the universities function.

The Constitution of India begins with the resolve to secure
equality of status and of opportunity. Equality of status in at least
the formal sense is easily secured by abolishing legally the privileges
and disabilities permanently associated with particular stations in
life. Equality of opportunity is a different matter altogether. Firstly,
it is difficult, if not impossible, to create full equality in the external

conditions of competition. Secondly, what equality of opportunity leads to is not equality but inequality of result. In 'Equality of Opportunity', which was the G. L. Mehta Memorial Lecture for 1982, I discuss the various ways in which the principle of equal opportunity may be regulated so as to reduce both the rewards and the penalties of competition.

It will be seen that the essays deal with a set of related problems, although there are both gaps and repetitions in the collection as a whole. Although I have made some changes here and there, I have left all the essays, except 'Harmonic and Disharmonic Social Systems', in more or less their original forms. Firstly, in preparing a collection of this kind, one has to think of the unity of each individual piece and not just of the whole collection. Secondly, I cannot say that I have come to any final conclusion regarding the problems I have discussed, and I have thought it best to leave the reader with some sense of the dilemmas involved in their solution.

The Idea of Natural Inequality*

The Auguste Comte Memorial Lecture, 1979

> The mind of man is far from the nature of a clear and equal glass,
> wherein the beams of things should reflect according to their true
> incidence: nay, it is rather like an enchanted glass, full of superstition
> and imposture . . .
>
> FRANCIS BACON

When we talk about inequality among men we mean various things.
We mean in one sense that human beings are unequally placed, that
they have unequal opportunities and that they are unequally rewarded; this kind of inequality is easily recognized and can easily
be shown to exist in any society, simple or complex, past or present.
But we also mean in another sense that men and women have unequal
abilities, that they are unequally endowed, and also perhaps that
they are of unequal worth; the proof of this kind of inequality is
difficult, one might say impossible.

Those who make the case for natural inequality will readily
concede that people sometimes appear to be unequally endowed
because in fact the opportunities available to them are unequal. No
society is perfect, and in every society some individuals suffer more
than others from a variety of contingent circumstances. But, they
will go on to argue, this is not all that there is to it. For, according
to them, it should be possible to remove the existing distortions or
imperfections, at least in principle, and when this is done we will
still be left with certain irreducible inequalities of endowment.
Viewed in this light the main problem of social justice is to bring

* A first sketch of the argument of this essay was presented at a conference in
Burg Wartenstein organized by the Wenner-Gren Foundation which I would like
to thank for its hospitality on that occasion. I am grateful to Marshall Sahlins for
his comments then. I am grateful also to Meyer Fortes, Edmund Leach and Alan
Macfarlane for their patience and care in reading and commenting on earlier
drafts of this essay.

about a strict correspondence between natural inequality and social inequality.

To an anthropologist, for whom the variety of cultures has a central place in the human scheme of things, it would appear that the idea of natural inequality is inherently ambiguous, if not a contradiction in terms. Nature presents us only with differences or potential differences. With human beings these differences do not become inequalities unless and until they are selected, marked out and evaluated by processes that are cultural and not natural. In other words, differences become inequalities only with the application of scales; and the scales with which we are concerned in talking about inequalities in a social context are not given to us by nature, but culturally constructed by particular human beings under particular historical conditions.

At the same time, the idea of natural inequality is a very durable one, and especially so in a competitive society. People like to believe that the inequalities they see around them—not all of them perhaps, but at least some—are in the nature of things.

It would be a mistake to suppose that such beliefs cannot coexist with the idealization of equality. There is surely something paradoxical about an age that seems to value equality as such, as an end in itself, and at the same time places so much faith in competition whose result can only be inequality. For no matter how scrupulously we ensure equality of opportunity, there can be equality only before the competition, not after it. Seen from this angle, equality of opportunity appears as the price paid by competitive societies to ensure inequality of reward.

The whole system of competition would lose its legitimacy unless people believed that the results of competition reveal or ought to reveal something basic and fundamental about those who engage in it. And the legitimacy of competition is very widely accepted in the advanced industrial societies, though in different ways in the capitalist and the socialist varieties. I would like to argue that there is in these societies a widespread belief, generally implicit, but sometimes explicit, that there is a natural ordering of individuals which is obscured by the institutions of primitive or traditional societies, and that this ordering can be revealed only through fair and free competition. The orders of rank which obtained in past societies might be capricious and arbitrary, but the one revealed by free and fair competition must correspond to the natural scheme of things.

The point I have in mind may be illustrated by referring to Tocqueville who believed that it was possible to abolish the privileges granted by law, but not those granted by nature.[1] Tocqueville sought to contrast aristocratic with democratic societies in terms of their morphology as well as their ideology. Democratic societies were based on the principle of equality just as aristocratic societies had been based on the principle of hierarchy. Tocqueville believed that, while there was something providential about humanity's progress towards equality, there were also certain limits, imposed by nature as it were, to the realization of this equality. This was obviously the case with the three principal races inhabiting the United States, but true as well of the individual members of the more favoured race.

It has been a commonplace since Tocqueville's time to connect equality with individualism. But, while it is commonly held that individualism entails equality,[2] the opposite argument can also be plausibly made. Individualism, when combined with a high value on achievement, creates and legitimizes a structure of unequal rewards. The very fact that individuals vary enormously in their achievement is presented as proof that they are unequally endowed. Indeed, there is a kind of finality about the order established by competition precisely to the extent that the competition is believed to be free and fair; for by this very belief people deny themselves the right of appeal in any other court. The unsuccessful are also inferior, demonstrably and conclusively so; and in a secular, competitive and achievement-oriented world, there can be little hope that their inferiority will be cancelled out in a life hereafter.

In modern industrial societies the economic domain is marked out as the pre-eminent arena of competition and individual achievement. And, as Sir Isaiah Berlin has put it, 'The unequal distribution of natural gifts is a well-known obstacle to economic equality.'[3] Even if we accept for the moment the idea of natural gifts, clearly not all such gifts have the same relevance to the achievement of economic success. Perhaps we may go a step further and say that while there is a variety of natural qualities, only some of these and not others

---

[1] A. de Tocqueville, *Democracy in America*, Alfred Knopf, 1956, vol. 2, pp. 38.

[2] See, for instance, L. Dumont, *From Mandeville to Marx: The Genesis and Triumph of Economic Ideology*, University of Chicago Press, 1977; also his *Homo Hierarchicus: The Caste System and Its Implications*, Paladin, 1972.

[3] I. Berlin, 'Equality' in his *Concepts and Categories: Philosophical Essays*, Hogarth Press, 1978, p. 92.

are transformed into gifts by the operation of the economic system itself.

Not all societies mark out the same qualities for favoured attention. Each society chooses from among the multitude of qualities with which human beings are endowed, or potentially endowed, only some, while ignoring others. The conventional character of gifts widely regarded as 'natural' is best revealed when we make comparisons between societies whose conventions are markedly different. Such enquiries are in fact the staple of comparative sociology. The difficulty in achieving satisfactory results in them arises from the fact that what is presented as comparative sociology is very often the comparison of all societies in terms of the implicit conventions of one. Nevertheless, comparative sociology, with all its limitations, has succeeded in revealing the 'artificial' character of most of what is or was considered 'natural' in non-Western societies, and also to some extent in Western society before the modern age.

A system of inequality whose artificial, not to say arbitrary, character is plainly revealed in the light of comparative sociology is the one associated with the Hindu order of castes. This system divided the whole of society into four *varnas* according to one scheme and into innumerable *jatis* according to another, both of which were characterized by a strict order of ranking. And yet, all of this, which appears so arbitrary from the outside, was believed by the Hindus to correspond to the natural order of things. It was given its rationale by the Hindu theory of *gunas* or qualities, according to which each individual was endowed with one of three basic qualities (or *gunas*), or some combination of them. In a just and stable society a correspondence was presumed between a person's qualities and his social position, but this correspondence might be disturbed by a variety of circumstances, in which case it was the duty of the just ruler to restore it.[4]

It is a far cry from the qualities esteemed among persons in a traditional hierarchical society to those that ensure success in examinations, let us say, or on the job market in an industrial society. There are differences between the two kinds of scales not only in their construction but also in the manner of their application. In the one case pre-eminence is assigned to birth, and in the other to competition. We know today that birth as such in a particular family or

[4] See, for instance, N. K. Bose, *The Structure of Hindu Society*, Orient Longman, 1975.

lineage tells us little about the natural qualities of human beings; but how much more does competition tell us? What I am suggesting is that something may be learnt by comparing the reasons people give in support of inequalities in hierarchical societies, with those they give in its support in competitive societies.[5]

The ambiguity underlying the distinction between natural inequality and social inequality is nowhere more evident than in Rousseau's celebrated discourse on Inequality. Others before him, notably English political philosophers like Hobbes and Locke, had stated that human beings were equal in their natural condition. Rousseau's case is the more interesting because, while he accepted the spirit of this proposition, he was not able to dispose of the idea of natural inequality altogether. It is useful to reconsider Rousseau's arguments because the questions he raised are still important questions, and the distinctions he made explicitly are still implicitly made.

In a general way the contrast is between 'the equality which nature has ordained between men' and the 'inequality which they have introduced'.[6] As one proceeds with the essay one finds Rousseau struggling to prove that natural inequalities do not really count, that every kind of inequality worth the name is social, not natural. Why then does he feel obliged to begin by making a distinction between natural or physical, and moral or political inequality? Again, why does he say that natural inequality is 'established by nature' whereas political inequality is 'established, or at least authorised by the consent of men'?[7] If political inequality is merely authorized by the consent of men, then how or by whom is it established?

It may be that, despite his moral commitment to equality, when it came to constructing a social world in his mind, Rousseau found it hard to conceive of all its individual components as being equal

[5] The contrast is by no means a very clear one. There are strongly hierarchical features in some competitive societies (of which contemporary Britain is a good example), and there is no human society, hierarchical or otherwise, from which competition has been fully excluded. Likewise, the contrast between 'birth' and 'competition' should not be overdrawn; those who are most strongly committed to competition might also believe that the results of competition are predetermined by birth, particularly for members of different races.

[6] J.-J. Rousseau, 'A Discourse on the Origin of Inequality' in *The Social Contract and Discourses*, J. M. Dent, 1938, p. 157.

[7] Ibid., p. 174.

in every respect. Many have pointed to the difficulty of creating such
a world even in imagination.[8] The simple solution seems to lie in
assuming that the individual human components were unequal to
begin with, i.e. before the construction of the social world began.
Rousseau, at any rate, leaves the door open for a wide range of such
pre-existing inequalities, arising, in his words, from differences in
'age, health, bodily strength and the qualities of the mind or of the
soul'.[9]

Does nature distribute her gifts unequally among men? Rousseau
seems to be in two minds about this. On the one hand, he wants to
show with almost tender care the even-handed character of nature's
bounty. On the other, he is eager to trace the steps through which
'the natural inequality of mankind' became greatly increased by 'the
inequality of social institutions'.[10] Further, it is not merely the great
increase of the latter over the former that is irksome, but also the
total lack of correspondence between them: the question of such
correspondence being, according to Rousseau, fit only 'to be discussed by slaves in the hearing of their masters'.[11] But, as we shall
see, it is this correspondence, real or presumed, that creates much of
the interest in the idea of natural inequality in the first place.

It appears that Rousseau is trying to prove two different propositions: firstly, that there is no correspondence, or no just correspondence between natural and social inequalities; and secondly,
that there are no significant natural inequalities, or even that there
are no natural inequalities as such among men. Now, one might
argue that if Rousseau were really convinced of the proof of the
second proposition, he would not need to prove the first. It might
well be asked whether Rousseau did not believe that at least the
different races of man were unequally endowed by nature.[12]

Rousseau seems to be talking at one and the same time about
(i) natural inequality among men, and (ii) inequality among men in
a state of nature. The former is possibly a wider conception than the
latter, but one gets very little help from Rousseau in forming a clear
idea of the distinction between the two. Presumably natural inequality among men can exist both in a state of nature and in a state
of society. And presumably one can argue about natural inequality

   [8] Berlin, 'Equality'.
   [9] Rousseau, 'A Discourse on the Origin of Inequality', p. 157.
   [10] Ibid., p. 204.   [11] Ibid., p. 174.
   [12] J. Baker, *Race*, Oxford University Press, 1974, pp. 16–17.

in a state of nature only in axiomatic terms, as facts 'do not affect the question'. But can one appeal to facts in talking about natural inequality in a state of society? What kinds of facts?

Again, the inequalities in a state of society are not all of the same kind. On the one hand, there are inequalities specific to the state of society, created by it and without any basis at all in the state of nature. On the other hand, the state of society magnifies and trans- forms, sometimes beyond recognition, natural inequalities that have been carried over into it from a prior state.

Rousseau's name has come to be inseparably linked with the French Revolution, and he has been hailed as an avatar of equality not only in Europe but in every country that has come under the influence of Western democratic ideals.[13] It may be said that what Rousseau was to the Revolution of 1789, Locke had been to that of 1688; at any rate, it would be difficult to exaggerate Locke's in- fluence on the development of democratic ideals in England and, more particularly, the United States. Locke's writings on equality and inequality in the state of nature, though narrower in scope than Rousseau's, are not themselves free from ambiguity.

Locke begins his *Second Treatise* by presenting the state of nature as a 'state also of equality',[14] and goes on to reiterate in various contexts 'the equality of men by nature'.[15] However, in talking about the subordination of the wife to the husband, he had said already in the *First Treatise* that 'there is, I grant, a foundation in Nature for it'.[16] And, later in a somewhat uncharacteristic passage on slaves, he says that they 'being captives taken in a just war are, by the right of Nature subjected to the absolute dominion and arbitrary power of their masters'.[17]

But more important are the qualifications that Locke specifically introduces to restrict his own general propositions about natural equality. 'Though I have said above (2) "That all men by nature are equal", I cannot be supposed to understand all sorts of "equality".'[18] The equality granted by nature is in fact to be understood in a

---

[13] For instance, his work inspired the nineteenth-century Bengali writer Bankimchandra Chatterji who wrote a tract on Equality in which he placed Rousseau (along with Christ and the Buddha) among the avatars of equality. For an English translation of Bankim's tract see M. K. Haldar, *Renaissance and Reaction in Nineteenth Century Bengal*, Minerva Associates (Calcutta), 1977.

[14] J. Locke, *Two Treatises of Government*, Dent, 1978, p. 118.

[15] Ibid., p. 119.   [16] Ibid., p. 34.   [17] Ibid., p. 158.

[18] Ibid., p. 142.

limited political sense, as the equal right of every man to his natural freedom without subjection to the arbitrary will or authority of any other man. Beyond this, nature acknowledges all kinds of distinctions, for 'Age or virtue may give men a just precedency. Excellency of parts and merit may place others above the common level.'[19] Locke makes no attempt to examine how distinctions of virtue or merit might arise in a state of nature, but simply leaves his reader to assume that they are there together with a certain equality of condition.

Perhaps we are today in a better position to recognize that the distinction between the state of nature and the state of society, or between nature and culture is not merely ambiguous, but inherently so. The difficulty lies not so much in getting at the facts as in the very act of conceptualizing man's nature independently of his culture. The recovery of this old insight by modern anthropology calls for a fresh examination of the presumed basis of inequality in human societies.

There are two broad ways in which social scientists represent inequality among people. They might try to show how certain valued items—whether possessions or qualities—are unequally distributed between individuals considered independently of any relations that might exist among them. Or, they might try to show how elements of inequality, such as deference, superordination, subordination, etc., are entailed in these very relations. This distinction corresponds to what I have elsewhere described as the distinction between the 'distributive' and the 'relational' aspects of inequality.[20] They both presuppose the existence of society and culture, although the former does so in a less obvious sense than the latter.

Let us consider first the inequalities entailed in the arrangement of individuals into some kind of an organized whole. If one took a set of blocks, one might find them to be either various in shape and unequal in size, or of exactly the same shape and size. If one took a set of blocks of exactly the same shape and size, one might arrange them in such a way that some are placed above and others below, without there being anything in the nature of the blocks themselves

[19] Ibid., p. 142.
[20] A. Béteille (ed.), *Social Inequality*, Penguin Books, 1969, p. 13; see also my *Inequality among Men*, Basil Blackwell, 1977.

Who is who 2 sc .

rep

to determine which ones should be placed above and which ones below. Now, if the blocks were human beings, they would need to find or be given reasons as to why some should be below and others above. I believe that many of the arguments about natural inequality are in fact a response to just this kind of problem. In other words, even if individuals were not naturally unequal, one might have to represent them as such in order to explain or justify their arrangement in an organized whole.

It is, in fact, quite common to view society in morphological terms, as being some kind of a whole comprising an ordered arrangement of parts. In this sense societies exist not only among humans, but also among various animal, notably insect, species. If this kind of order is a necessary condition for the existence of such a society— any society, whether human or animal—then are the inequalities entailed by the order natural or not? There is no reason to believe with either Rousseau or Hobbes that the division of labour and the state of nature are antithetical to each other.

The problem is somewhat simpler in the case of non-human species such as ants, bees and termites where there is morphological differentiation within the species corresponding to its division of labour. Further, whether simple or elaborate, the division of labour is clear and unambiguous, and the same pattern is replicated from one colony to the next within the species. These two features in combination give such division of labour a fixed and unalterable appearance.

In the human species there is no obvious correspondence between morphological differentiation and the division of labour. The two most manifest forms of morphological differentiation are those that relate to race and to sex. Even if it turns out that the various races are variously endowed, there is no self-evident way of matching racial differentiation with the division of labour; in any case, the division of labour is no less a problem in racially homogeneous societies than it is in racially heterogeneous ones. And, as it is becoming increasingly clear, the biological components of sex provide only the broadest limits within which an almost endless variety of social arrangements is possible.

One important aspect of the division of labour among human beings, an aspect that is related to its variability as well as its flexibility, is that those who participate in it require reasons for its existence. Human beings do not in any society simply fit themselves into the division of labour as they find it; they seek or create reasons that explain or justify it. From this point of view the division of labour among human beings differs from that among animals, probably as much as human language differs from animal language.

The division of labour as it exists in any human society entails certain inequalities of status and power among the differentiated parts or positions. Some positions are more highly esteemed or command more authority than others. Sometimes, as in the Hindu *varna* system, the whole of society is divided up into categories that are serially ordered. Two kinds of arguments are characteristically put forward today to explain or justify such differentiation: firstly, that in its essence it represents the division of labour and not inequality, and secondly, that the division of labour as such corresponds to the natural scheme of things. These in fact were the arguments of Mahatma Gandhi who may be regarded as the most important modern interpreter of Hinduism. Indeed, Gandhi's argument was that the division of labour corresponding to *varnashrama* is natural, hence good, whereas the division of labour corresponding to class is artificial, hence evil.

Gandhi was not the only person to argue that social differentiation in his own society represented the division of labour rather than inequality. Soviet sociologists too maintain that the differentiation of their society into peasants, workers and the intelligentsia represents the division of labour which they are inclined to contrast with class. Inequalities associated with class are exploitative, and can and should be removed; the division of labour, on the other hand, corresponds to the natural conditions of social existence.

The authors of the *The German Ideology* were much closer to the original insight of Rousseau when they argued that the division of labour, class and inequality are inseparably linked. Indeed, their argument is more fully developed on this point than Rousseau's. At least in this early phase of their work they saw no real solution to the problems of class and inequality so long as there was division of labour in society. But they did not concede that the division of labour was a necessary condition of social existence; rather, they believed that human society would recover its true nature only when the division of labour was abolished.[21]

Is the argument of Marx and Engels in *The German Ideology*

[21] K. Marx and F. Engels, *The German Ideology*, Progress Publishers, 1968, p. 93.

tenable that the division of labour is not a necessary (or 'natural') condition of social existence? I believe that it is not, although there is something very persuasive about such an argument. Its appeal seems to rest largely on the obvious fact that among humans, unlike among insects, the division of labour is endlessly variable in both space and time. But to argue that this particular form of the division of labour—any particular form of it—is dispensable (or 'artificial') is very different from arguing that the division of labour itself is dispensable.

There is from this point of view a certain likeness between the division of labour and language. No human society is conceivable without some division of labour just as none is conceivable without a language. At the same time, no particular form of either the one or the other can be stipulated as a necessary condition for the existence of society. People are now prepared to concede that their own language is no more natural than any other language, although they have not always or everywhere been prepared to do so. It seems far more difficult for them to be reconciled to a similar view of the division of labour to which they are accustomed.

The division of labour among men and women, and their ordering on a scale, however closely related, are not one and the same thing. It should be possible to order individual items on a scale without there being any pre-existing pattern of arrangement among them. In fact, those who talk about inequality among men, particularly natural inequality, do not necessarily presuppose any division of labour among them. Is it possible to order individual human beings without their social division of labour—rights, obligations, shared values—being at all taken into account? By what criteria should one test the adequacy of such ordering?

The basic question centres around the autonomy of the scales that are used for representing or identifying the inequalities among people. If these scales are themselves embedded in the existing social arrangements, then there is an element of fiction involved in the belief that the inequalities they represent are natural as opposed to social.

There obviously is some sense in making a distinction between inequality of merit and inequality of reward, and in pointing out that merit does not always receive its due reward. These are practical problems that concern individuals in every society. But one may wonder whether we clarify or confuse the issue by arguing as if the first (i.e. merit) were a creation of nature and the second (i.e. reward) an artefact of culture. It is misleading to believe that only the allocation of rewards is a social process; the recognition of merit—and indeed the very definition of what constitutes merit—is equally and as much a social process.

It is the common experience that human beings discriminate and evaluate everywhere, ordering things and persons on scales of various kinds. We do not know very much about the ways in which these scales are constructed, except that they are somehow related to collective experience, and, more particularly, to what Durkheim described as collective representations. Some scales evidently are constructed by particular persons for particular purposes, and we can see their 'artificial' character easily enough. But there are others which we accept without question, on which there is complete or almost complete agreement within a society because of long usage or for some other reason: do they then enjoy the special privilege of being beyond the realm of culture?

It would appear that there are such layers in every system of collective representations: those criteria, measures and standards of evaluation that are tacitly accepted as being 'natural', and others whose 'artificial' or man-made character is freely conceded. But it is hard to see how discrimination and evaluation of any kind can operate independently of culture. Conversely, it is hard to conceive of a culture which does not discriminate or evaluate, just as it is hard to conceive of a society which has no division of labour. So that we may say that it is in the nature of every culture to order things on its own scales; which is another way of saying that the distinction between 'natural' inequality and 'social' inequality is inherently ambiguous.

I would like at this point to briefly consider the argument of Mahatma Gandhi about equality and inequality in the context of the natural capacities of individual human beings. I do not expect that you will find it any more convincing than I do. Rather, Gandhi's argument that a particular social arrangement expresses or can express differences of natural ability will be found paradoxical precisely because it is presented in the idiom of another culture.

Gandhi, who commented extensively on Hinduism as well as other religions, was inclined to view the contrast between Hindu society based on *varnashrama* and capitalist society based on classes as a contrast between the natural (or organic) and the artificial (or mechanical). He maintained that the division of society into the four *varnas* of Brahmin, Kshatriya, Vaishya and Shudra was in accordance with the natural order of things, whereas a division into classes whose members were in perpetual competition with each other was the artefact of a mechanical civilization. The first, though corrupt in its current practice, was inherently good; the second was inherently evil because it obstructed the expression of man's real nature.

Gandhi maintained that in *varnadharma* the Hindus had discovered a law of collective life given to man by nature: 'It is not a human invention, but an immutable law of nature.'[22] As such, it ought to be the organizing principle not merely of Hindu society but of every human society.

> Though the law of *Varna* is a special discovery of some Hindu seer, it has universal application. Every religion has some distinguishing characteristic, but if it expresses a principle or law, it ought to have universal application. This is how I look at the law of *Varna*. The world may ignore it today but it will have to accept it in the time to come.[23]

In fairness, it ought to be said that Gandhi's conception of *varna* was very different from the representation of it that we get in the usual text-book of sociology.

What is *varna*? The law of *varna*, according to the argument, simply enjoins individual human beings to follow the traditional callings of their forefathers in a spirit of duty and service. Gandhi recognized the connection between *varna* and birth, but he did not regard that as a point against it.[24] This may sound strange because Gandhi, like Rousseau, was a radical egalitarian. He condemned caste, but endorsed *varna*, because, according to him, 'All Varnas are equal, for the community depends no less on one than on another.'[25] Gandhi argued that feelings of superiority and inferiority were a perversion of *varnadharma*, and inconsistent with its basic spirit.

Feelings of superiority and inferiority are inherent in the competitive society, and from this point of view class distinctions are rooted not so much in property as in competition, individualism and

[22] M. K. Gandhi, *Varnashramadharma*, Navjivan Publishing House, 1962, p. 13.
[23] Ibid., p. 8.   [24] Ibid., p. 6.   [25] Ibid., p. 7.

the unlimited pursuit of material gain. As such, they are present
under both private and state capitalism. Gandhi's hostility to the
dominance of the machine over man is well known. He believed that
so long as this dominance prevailed man would remain enmeshed in
artificial distinctions and inequalities, unable to recover his true
nature as a social being.

In contrast to all this, nineteenth-century Western liberals and
their present-day counterparts maintain that the natural ordering
among men can be established and maintained only through fair
and free competition. (See references to Durkheim and to Davis and
Moore below.) If this ordering reveals inequality, then inequality is to
that extent natural, and to suppress such inequality might be to go
against both justice and efficiency. Other principles might be invoked
to mitigate natural inequality, but one cannot, and indeed should
not, cancel it out.

It is not as if there is no awareness in the advanced industrial
societies of the negative consequences of unrestricted competition.
This awareness has steadily grown over the last hundred years, and
has led to the introduction of a variety of measures to ensure that
society maintains a floor and a ceiling beyond which people do not
easily fall or rise. But these measures do not in principle negate the
belief that unequal rewards are inevitable in a world in which natural
gifts are unequally distributed. Even in the East European countries
social scientists are eager to show that the meritarian principle of
remuneration is not really in conflict with the socialist principle.[26]

In the West the nineteenth century ushered in a new social order
and a new consciousness; and, along with these, new hopes and new
fears. Tocqueville foresaw the levelling of the old distinctions between
high and low, and the emergence of a new spirit of equality among
men. Marx, who took a closer look at this new society with its
inhuman division of labour and its brutal competition, argued that
the age of equality would come only with the dissolution, not the
consolidation of the new social order.

A new concentration of intellectual energy was required to make
the commitment to equality on one plane consistent with the commitment to inequality on another. Writing in the last decade of the

[26] For instance, W. Wesolowski and T. Krauze, 'Socialist Society and the
Meritocratic Principle of Remuneration' in G. D. Berreman (ed.), *Social Inequality: Comparative and Developmental Approaches*, Academic Press, 1981,
pp. 337–49.

nineteenth century, Émile Durkheim reacted to the paradox of his time in a characteristic manner. He noted, on the one hand, the growing belief among citizens—one might ask, which citizens?— about the increase of equality; and, on the other, the inherent tendency of the division of labour to lead to the increase of inequality.[27] How did he seek to resolve the paradox? Durkheim did not deny that the division of labour might lead to the increase of inequality; only, he maintained that such inequality, when established by free competition, would be just and efficient.

Durkheim, like Tocqueville, was struck by the contrast between the *ancien régime* and the new society. But between Tocqueville and Durkheim lay the work of Marx, and it was no longer possible to present the contrast between the old and the new orders as simply a contrast between hierarchy and equality. One was now obliged to argue that it did not matter that the new order too had its inequality, and that this inequality might in fact increase. What mattered was that the new inequality, quite unlike the old, gave due recognition to merit. But what is merit?

There was, to begin with, the entire panoply of hereditary titles, ranks and offices whose oppressive and artificial character stood clearly revealed in the light of the new social consciousness. Durkheim had no difficulty in showing that merit, as he and his readers understood it, would be stifled and not given an opportunity to develop as long as the old distinctions of estate, of caste and of clan prevailed. The hopeful thing was that these were being steadily and surely effaced as the new division of labour gained ground. But when these became fully effaced, would true merit really come into its own and get its due recognition? What was there to guarantee that, when the veil of artificial social distinctions was removed, a social order based solely on true distinctions of merit would emerge?

Durkheim was a product of the society that first established the myth of careers open to talent, a myth whose power has been on the whole increased rather than diminished by the resources of modern science. It was a society that set great store by merit, viewing merit to be somewhat like water which, when left to itself, always finds its own level. The task of social reconstruction lay then in removing the obstacles to the free play of merit, so that a 'forced' division of labour could be replaced by a 'spontaneous' division of labour; and a society

[27] É. Durkheim, *The Division of Labour in Society*, The Free Press, 1933; see in particular the chapter on 'The Forced Division of Labour'.

that put common faith above everything else could be replaced by one that put justice above everything else. But what is justice without a common faith?

Durkheim's idea of the just society then is not that it is one in which all men are equal in every way, or even that it is one in which the inequalities among them are small in extent; as we saw, he believed that the new division of labour might lead inequalities to increase rather than decrease.[28] His idea of the just society is simply that it is one in which 'social inequalities exactly express natural inequalities'.[29] But Durkheim, who is otherwise so careful to explain the social origin of everything, including freedom and justice, does not really explain where these natural inequalities come from. They are simply taken to be the fixed points with reference to which the just society—the society that puts justice above common faith—regulates its inequalities. But what if these 'natural inequalities' are themselves the creatures of the very society that is presumed merely to express them?

The kind of problem that all this raises—and leaves unresolved—is very well illustrated by the notorious Functionalist Theory of Social Stratification. According to this theory, presented in its simplest form by Kingsley Davis and Wilbert Moore,[30] the rewards allotted to individuals are roughly in proportion to the contributions they make to society. Since the theory proposes no independent measures of the values of these contributions, it is in fact perfectly circular. But although the Functionalist Theory of Stratification has been ruled out of court by professional sociologists on account of its circularity, it has scarcely been dislodged from its place of importance in the folk wisdom of modern societies.

The problem of an independent measure of ability, merit or talent is of course the central problem left unresolved in the conception of natural inequality to which Durkheim and others like him take

---

[28] As Adam Smith had pointed out before him: '. . . the very different genius which appears to distinguish men of different professions, when grown up to maturity, is not upon many occasions so much the cause, as the effect of the division of labour. The difference between the most dissimilar characters, between a philosopher and a common street porter, for example, seems to arise not so much from nature, as from habit, custom, and education.' *The Wealth of Nations*, University of Chicago Press, 1967, p. 19.

[29] Durkheim, *The Division of Labour in Society*, p. 377.

[30] The debate has been reproduced in R. Bendix and S. M. Lipset (eds.), *Class, Status and Power: A Comparative Perspective*, The Free Press, second edition, 1966.

recourse. Suppose for a moment that there are natural inequalities among individuals: by what means are we to determine the degree of correspondence between these and the existing social inequalities? Can the correspondence between the two be subjected to any kind of empirical test? No one has come anywhere near to constructing such a test for any society in its totality, and it is doubtful that we even know what kinds of data would be relevant to such a test.

Instead of starting with a system of natural inequality out there, and then trying to see how society adjusts its positions to correspond to it, suppose we were to start with the order and its existing social inequalities. Would the order then not have to give reason as to why particular individuals are placed where they are, and not elsewhere? Is there anything more to the presumed correspondence between 'natural' and 'social' inequality than just this reason? Suppose there were no natural inequality among men, would society not need to invent it? And would the need for this invention be less compelling in a competitive than in a hierarchical society?

The need for a belief in natural inequality has perhaps a special urgency in a modern secular society where people can no longer pretend that the inequalities in this world are unreal or unimportant, since they might be cancelled out in a world hereafter. In such a society the individual is given only one chance, as it were, to find his true place in the larger scheme of things. So it is not altogether surprising that the resources of modern science should be used for buttressing the concept of natural inequality, even though the concept is inherently ambiguous.

The science that in the nineteenth century contributed most to the support of folk beliefs about natural inequality was biology. What is interesting about this biology is the extent to which, in dealing with the question of human nature, it took for granted the categories of the society of which it was a product. The sociobiology and the bioeconomics of the second half of the present century have become enormously more complex and technical, but it is doubtful that they have succeeded any more in detaching themselves from the categories of a competitive and market-oriented society.[31]

In the closing years of the last century T. H. Huxley published a

[31] For a stimulating recent discussion see M. Sahlins, *The Use and Abuse of Biology: An Anthropological Critique of Sociobiology*, Tavistock Publications, 1977.

magazine article 'On the Natural Inequality of Men'.[32] The article
was an attack on Rousseau's discourse on Inequality, and carried
behind it the whole weight of the author's reputation as one of
Britain's leading scientists. Huxley attacked Rousseau for being
both inconsistent and disingenuous; he pointed out, moreover, that
every one of Rousseau's basic ideas might be traced back to either
Locke or Hobbes.

Huxley made no secret of his antipathy for unqualified equality:
'Freedom, used foolishly, and equality, asserted in words, but every
moment denied by the facts of nature, are things of which, as it seems
to me, we have rather too much already.'[33] Equality was sanctioned
neither by science nor by philosophy; even the equality sanctioned
by the great religions, Judaism and Christianity, was a residual kind,
'an equality either of insignificance or of imperfection'.[34]

Unlike Rousseau, Huxley was convinced that there was a close
correspondence between natural inequality and social inequality.
The proof of this lay in the evident success of enterprise and skill in
every walk of life. Enterprise and skill, moreover, accounted for
property rights as they prevailed in nineteenth-century Britain: 'so
the inequality of individual ownership has grown out of the relative
equality of communal ownership in virtue of those natural inequalities of men, which, if unimpeded by circumstances, cannot fail to
give rise quietly and peaceably to corresponding political inequalities.'[35] Echoes of Huxley's words are to be found in the writings of a
large number of his contemporaries.[36]

Enterprise and skill were viewed as the basis of property accumulation and occupational achievement, the twin pillars on which
nineteenth-century capitalist society rested. Huxley's essay was an
attempt to show that the inequalities which fuelled the engines of
that society were in fact a part of the quiet and peaceable order of
nature. There has been a certain shift since his time to the extent that
more emphasis appears to be placed now on the natural basis of
occupational achievement than of property accumulation.

The arguments Huxley set forth in a magazine article were pre-

[32] T. H. Huxley, 'On the Natural Inequality of Men', *The Nineteenth Century*,
No. CLV (January 1890), pp. 1–23.   [33] Ibid., p. 12.

[34] Ibid., p. 13; for a recent statement of the same argument see K. Joseph and
J. Sumption, *Equality*, John Murray, 1979.

[35] Ibid., p. 22.

[36] Among contemporary writers perhaps the most notorious is H. J. Eysenck,
The Inequality of Man, Fontana, 1975.

sented in scientific treatises by Sir Francis Galton who in the nine-teenth century laid the groundwork for that field of studies which examines the relationship between biological heredity and social achievement. Galton had been greatly struck by the unequal achieve-ments of individuals in various walks of life, and sought to prove that much of this was due to heredity. I am not here concerned with show-ing how far Galton was right or wrong within his own framework of analysis; my concern is with the presuppositions of that framework. And Galton's work is important precisely because it makes little effort to conceal those presuppositions.

Galton begins his book on *Hereditary Genius*, first published in 1869, with the magisterial statement, 'It is in the most unqualified manner that I object to pretensions of natural equality.'[37] And what is the evidence to sustain his objection? He quickly proceeds to provide his most persuasive piece of evidence, which is as follows: 'There can hardly be a surer evidence of the enormous difference between the intellectual capacity of men, than the prodigious dif-ference in the number of marks obtained by those who gain mathe-matical honours at Cambridge.'[38] Later in the same work Galton substitutes, for purely technical reasons, success in the classical tripos for success in the mathematical tripos as evidence of superior natural ability.

Galton's line of reasoning seems to be that natural inequalities result in unequal success in examinations which requires that people be unequally placed in society: natural inequality is the bedrock on which all inequalities rest. He does not pause to consider the op-posite line of reasoning which might be that men and women have to be certified as naturally unequal because the examination system guarantees their unequal success, and the examination system is what it is because the larger society requires it to be so. On this last point a distinguished contemporary English academic has observed:

> If society insists that individuals be segregated out into categories
> —first class, second class, third class, upper, middle, lower—then
> the system will always have to waste an enormous amount of time
> and energy allocating individuals to the right slots and marking
> them up with the proper labels.[39]

[37] F. Galton, *Hereditary Genius*, Watts & Co., 1950, p. 12.
[38] Ibid., p. 14.
[39] E. Leach, *A Runaway World?*, The British Broadcasting Corporation, 1968, p. 73.

In this other perspective one sees what is ordinarily described as natural inequality to be largely an artefact of social inequality.

What is striking in Galton, in contrast to his contemporary counterparts, is his disarming candour. Durkheim would argue at most that there was in his society a tendency for social inequalities to express natural inequalities, not that they did so in fact. Galton, on the other hand, took the correspondence between the two for granted: 'It follows that the men who achieve eminence, and those who are naturally capable, are, to a large extent, identical.'[40] Further, men not only get what they deserve, their deserts are publicly acknowledged: 'I feel convinced that no man can achieve a very high reputation without being gifted with very high abilities.'[41] With so much trust in the existing system of social rewards, it would take a lot to disturb one's faith in natural inequality.

Nineteenth-century ideas regarding merit, talent or ability tended to be on the whole diffuse and ill-defined. The twentieth century has seen organized and concentrated efforts to make these terms more specific and concrete. There would be little point in talking about careers open to talent if one had only a vague idea of the meaning of talent. The answer to this appears to have been in large measure found in the quality that has come to be identified as intelligence, in particular, intelligence as measured by IQ. As a recent study entitled *American Beliefs and Attitudes About Intelligence* says,

> Still, it is true that measured intelligence today is of higher significance than ever before. . . . In our society there is an increasing value placed on measured intelligence as the basis on which rewards will be allocated, in preference to other characteristics such as honesty, creativity, altruism, leadership, and dramatic, painting, dancing or gardening skills.[42]

This is not to say that other qualities are no longer valued, but only that intelligence has come to acquire a kind of pre-eminence.

It is difficult not to be impressed by the inputs that have gone into the definition and discussion of intelligence. Psychologists, educationists, biologists and others have spoken and written about it at length. Scientific skills and political passions have been called into play, together with perhaps a small ingredient of fraud. It is doubtful that any other human quality has been so thoroughly discussed as

[40] Galton, *Hereditary Genius*, p. 34.   [41] Ibid., p. 43.
[42] O. G. Brim Jr., D. C. Glass, J. Neulinger and I. L. Firestone, *American Beliefs and Attitudes about Intelligence*, Russel Sage Foundation, 1969, p. 3.

intelligence, and implicit in much of the discussion is the belief that intelligence is a gift of nature, perhaps her supreme gift.

It is important to appreciate the extent of the preoccupation with intelligence and the testing of intelligence in the modern world. In this, as in so much else, the United States leads the field. Tests of ability have been standardized, and the number of such tests administered each year has grown phenomenally since the War. It was estimated in the mid-sixties that around 250 million standardized tests of ability were administered each year in the American school system.[43] In a society where schooling is both compulsory and competitive no child can escape having his intelligence tested, directly and indirectly, overtly and covertly, over and over again.

Nor is this all solely for the benefit of children. For the adult the popular press and the other mass media advertise the manifest virtues of intelligence, and there is now a scientific best-seller which invites people to check their own IQ.[44] More and more adults take standardized tests of intelligence because they are required to do so in almost every walk of life, in commerce, in industry, in the civil and military branches of government, and, of course, in education.[45] In addition to all this, individuals might administer such tests to themselves in order to keep themselves better informed about their own abilities. A student of comparative sociology might well ask if the notorious Brahminical obsession with purity can really measure up to this kind of preoccupation with a single human quality.

What makes intelligence particularly appropriate as a quality for the ranking of individuals is the belief that it can be precisely measured; or, rather, precise measures must be found for any quality if it is to satisfy the requirement of ranking individuals and classes in a modern society. As a result, the experts know much more about measuring intelligence than about what intelligence is. To put it in the words of Arthur Jensen, 'Intelligence, like electricity, is easier to measure than to define.'[46] For most people, in fact, the measure acts as a substitute for understanding, giving them the illusion that by measuring something they bring it within their grasp.

In modern societies achievement and ability are very closely

[43] Ibid., p. 1.
[44] H. J. Eysenck, *Check Your Own IQ*, Penguin Books, 1966.
[45] Brim et al., *American Beliefs and Attitudes about Intelligence*, p. 1.
[46] A. R. Jensen, 'How Much Can We Boost IQ and Scholastic Achievement?', *Harvard Educational Review*, Reprint Series No. 2, 1965, p. 5.

linked together. Achievement is the measure of ability, and ability is reckoned not in the abstract, but in relation to specific standards of achievement. These standards of achievement have their loci in various institutional systems, among which the two most crucial are the educational system and the occupational system. Modern societies are thus most concerned with those variations in human ability which have a direct bearing on scholastic and occupational achievement.

We must appreciate that those, like Arthur Jensen, who argue that heredity contributes substantially to differences in IQ readily concede this. Jensen is careful to make a distinction between 'intelligence', which is a narrower concept, and mental ability which is somewhat wider, pointing out that 'intelligence' as measured by intelligence tests is a specific set of abilities, marked out from among the rest because of its correspondence with the traditional system of formal education on the one hand and the established occupational structure on the other. In his own words, 'the predominant importance of intelligence is derived, not from any absolute criteria or God-given desiderata, but from social demands.'[47] Thus, inequalities here are measured neither on God's scale nor on nature's, but on scales constructed by men with particular ends in view. At the same time, and despite what the experts set down in fine print, these tests strongly confirm folk beliefs about natural inequality as being the basis of social inequality as represented by the occupational system.

Sociologists have, in their turn, pointed to the 'functional' properties of the quality conceived of as intelligence in modern intelligence tests; in particular, properties that make it functional to the requirements of the occupational system which, since Durkheim's time, has come to be recognized as the principal locus of prestige in modern societies. This is how one recent sociological study sums it up:

> What we call 'occupational prestige' corresponds to an unmistakable social fact. When psychologists came to propose operational counterparts to the notion of intelligence, or to derive measures thereof, they wittingly or unwittingly looked for indicators of capability to function in the system of key roles in society. What they took to be mental performance might equally well have been described as role performance.[48]

[47] Ibid., p. 19.
[48] O. D. Duncan, D. L. Featherman and B. Duncan, *Socioeconomic Background and Achievement*, Seminar Press, 1972, p. 78.

There is, as one might expect, a strain towards consistency between ability and achievement, or between quality and performance, both of which are socially defined, although the one tends to be thought of as natural in opposition to the other.

It is hardly surprising that psychologists concerned with intelligence ratings and sociologists concerned with the rating of occupations should come out with findings that are in such close agreement with each other. Occupations which rank high in a specific society and the specific abilities required for the performance of those occupations may be seen as two sides of the same coin. Intelligence ratings and occupational ratings are both socially constructed, and are in effect two different applications of the same basic scale. Now, if mental ability be considered as nature's gift and occupational standing as society's reward, it is only to be expected that social inequalities will express natural inequalities.

Recent debates on IQ have paid much attention to the relative contributions of heredity and environment to it. Most intelligence testers seem to believe that heredity has a far larger share than environment in determining IQ, although some disagree very sharply.[49] I ought to make it clear that I consider this to be a separate question from the one to which I have tried to address myself.

My argument is not about the fact of individual variations among human beings which are universal and undeniable, but about the significance of these variations. It is difficult to see how one can deny some role to genetic factors in the perpetuation of individual variations. As soon as some of these variations are marked out and transformed into inequalities by being ordered on a scale, such inequalities come rightly to be regarded as hereditary. It is the crucial step by which differences are transformed into inequalities that I consider to be a social construction rather than a gift of nature. What I have tried to argue, therefore, is that intelligence ratings are no more natural than occupational ratings, and when people talk about social inequalities expressing natural inequalities, they are making use of a fiction which even the most acute among them tend to mistake for the truth.

What I have tried to show above is that in modern societies there is characteristically a tension between the values placed on equality

[49] See, for instance, L. J. Kamin, *The Science and Politics of IQ*, Lawrence Erlbaum Associates, 1974.

and on inequality. There is, on the one hand, a strong and somewhat self-consciously virtuous attachment to equality, as in the principle of equal opportunity or of equal consideration of human worth. There is, on the other, a striking preoccupation with sorting individuals out and ranking them according to their natural abilities, aptitudes and qualities. These two concerns coexist not only within the same culture but often, and perhaps characteristically, within the same personality.

It would be difficult, if not impossible, to assign weights to these two different, and in some sense contradictory, concerns. For one thing, there are enormous variations between individuals within the same society, and between societies that have equal claims to modernity. One important difference seems to lie in the ways in which two modern societies, e.g. England and America, might articulate or give expression to these two contradictory concerns. On the whole the concern for equality is made more widely explicit whereas the one for inequality is more often left implicit, although here also one may find a good deal of fluctuation, including short-term fluctuation within the life history of the same society.[50]

On the whole people seem reluctant to declare categorically that human beings are by nature made unequal even when that is the implication of much of what they say. Because the idea of natural inequality is weakly articulated, it is never free from an element of ambiguity. The student of modern societies can follow people in what they say about their belief in equality, but he has to reconstruct their concept of natural inequality. It can be said that the concept of natural inequality owes some of its strength to its ambiguity since it enables one to shift from one sense of the term to another in arguing with others or with oneself.

It is not at all clear that when Berlin talks about 'the unequal distribution of natural gifts' he has in mind exactly the same sort of thing as when Galton rejects what he describes as 'pretensions to natural equality'. When pressed to the point people will often say that what they have in mind is not natural inequality in any absolute sense, but natural inequality relative to a given social arrangement. There is, as it were, a strong thesis about natural inequality and a weak thesis, and people tend to move back and forth between the two. The same person, A. R. Jensen, for instance, might caution his

---

[50] For a recent attack on egalitarianism by a leading member of the British cabinet see Joseph and Sumption, *Equality*.

readers that mental tests measure very specific, culturally-valued abilities, and then go on to refer to 'g' or generalized intelligence as the 'rock of Gibraltar'.[51]

A common source of the ambiguity referred to above is the tendency to move, back and forth, from arguments about natural difference to arguments about natural inequality and vice versa. The following is a characteristic example from an essay entitled 'The Inequality of Man' by J. B. S. Haldane: 'For men are not born equal. No one disputes this fact as regards physical characteristics. Some babies are born black and some white, and very little can be done to alter the colour of the former.'[52] From here one moves on to unequal competence in role performance and argues, by analogy, that these *inequalities*, like the *differences* between black and white babies, are due to nature and not nurture. If the reader feels a little confused as to what exactly is being ascribed to nature, that does not necessarily shake his belief in natural inequality.

What Haldane does with the example of black and white babies is to show that some differences are unalterable in order to suggest that some inequalities as well are unalterable, hence natural. What I have tried to show, on the other hand, is that examples of unalterable difference, however numerous or ingenious, cannot by themselves establish any argument about natural inequality. It is not as if Haldane is unaware that the difference between black and white babies might vary in significance from one culture to another. Rather, he moves on to examples of other differences which lend themselves more easily to the suggestion that their significance cannot but be the same, no matter what the society or culture is.

The view that the incontestable proof of natural inequality lies in the fact that some differences, of both physical and mental qualities, are hereditary, Haldane has himself elsewhere jocularly described as 'scientific Calvinism'.[53] The problem is that Calvinism, in both its religious and scientific forms, tends to be strict and narrow in the choice of the qualities it values. Perhaps the very narrowness helps to confirm the view that the choice itself is made for man by nature.

To represent what is socially constructed as something given to

[51] See Jensen, 'How Much Can We Boost IQ and Scholastic Achievement?', p. 9; also L. Hudson, *The Cult of the Fact*, Jonathan Cape, 1976.

[52] J. B. S. Haldane, 'The Inequality of Man' in J. B. S. Haldane, *The Inequality of Man and Other Essays*, Chatto and Windus, 1932, p. 13.

[53] J. B. S. Haldane, 'Scientific Calvinism', ibid., pp. 27–42.

man by nature is, according to Roland Barthes, the essence of the art of myth making.[54] The important thing is to seek an anchorage for the social and the historical in something outside of society and history, and that is the broad sense people give to nature when they talk about natural inequality. This being the case, it is not surprising that the idea resists rigorous definition. Myths, as opposed to theories, make their impact less by what they state explicitly than by what they persuade people to take for granted. Two hundred and fifty million test scores serve to make a point more effectively than any formal theory of natural inequality could hope to do.

If the idea of natural inequality has a somewhat shadowy existence, this is because it has little independent value in itself; its value lies in the anchorage it provides, or seeks to provide, to the reality of social inequality. If there had been no social inequality to contend with, it is doubtful that people would give very much thought to natural inequality. From this point of view Rousseau's professed lack of interest in the correspondence between the two forms or aspects of inequality does appear a little disingenuous, and T. H. Huxley was certainly right in pointing to the hollowness of his rhetoric.

The idea of natural inequality seems to have a special place in the modern world. It is perhaps best viewed as a response to the recognition of the transitoriness and the fragility of existing forms of social inequality. Modern societies appear to be animated by the urge to recreate themselves again and again. Through this process modern man seems to recognize instinctively that inequality is an inherent feature of collective life, and at the same time that any particular form of its social expression is not only oppressive but also arbitrary. But if the idea of natural inequality offers some kind of a refuge from the implications of this paradox, it is at best a precarious refuge.

[54] R. Barthes, *Mythologies*, Paladin, 1973.

Homo Hierarchicus, Homo Equalis

The Kingsley Martin Memorial Lecture, 1979

I would like to pay my tribute to the memory of Kingsley Martin by calling into question a part of the conventional wisdom of what passes for comparative sociology. I hope I will not appear unduly contentious in doing so. I would not like to speak badly of comparative sociology. At the same time, it has to be admitted that a truly comparative sociology exists less in the work that scholars actually do than in the ideals they profess. The principal obstacle to its growth is, in my opinion, neither lack of wit nor lack of words: it is prejudice.

The part of conventional wisdom to which I refer is the one by which a kind of sweeping contrast is encouraged between entire societies in terms of their univocal commitment to the principle of equality or its opposite. Some societies are seen to be animated by the spirit of hierarchy, and in these hierarchy is shown to permeate every sphere of life, from the family to the state. Others are shown to have an equally zealous attachment to the principle of equality, and where inequalities exist in these societies, they are explained, or explained away, as being marginal or residual, or as belonging to the domain of mere facts rather than of values.

In this contrast the exemplar of hierarchy is Indian society in particular and Oriental society in general, just as the exemplar of equality is Western society in general and American society in particular. The contrast, I must repeat, is not directed to the mere fact of inequality in the distribution of this or that resource; such inequality is freely acknowledged to exist in both types of society. It is rather a contrast between societies in terms of their principles of organization, their basic designs or the fundamental structures underlying their cultures.

The terms of the contrast are not in every regard symmetrical. Sociologists of the Western world, who are the main practitioners of comparative sociology, have, as one might expect, diverse attitudes towards their own society; which means that we get a more differentiated picture of Western society than of any other. The view that Western society is in its spirit egalitarian, though the dominant view, has never passed unchallenged in the West. On the other hand, Western intellectuals are satisfied with a less differentiated view of other societies. Thus, though the contrast between India and the West is not made equally sharply in every case, it is always made in the same way.

It is sometimes said that 'hierarchy' is a technical term, and should not be taken to mean the same thing as inequality in the simple sense. But to define a term rigorously is one thing, and to apply it consistently, particularly in the comparative study of complex societies, is another. At any rate, the idea of hierarchy entails that of inequality, whether we speak of a hierarchy of castes or of a hierarchy of angels. And in the context of the study of Indian society, past as well as present, it has come to signify not just inequality, but inequality of the most rigid and uncompromising kind. This impression is naturally strengthened when one talks not just of hierarchical society, but, no doubt for more dramatic effect, of hierarchical man, *homo hierarchicus* and contrasts him with *homo equalis*.

Someone who grew up in an India that was still a colony of Britain is not likely to be easily convinced that *homo hierarchicus* is uniquely Indian or that the European is the essence of *homo equalis*. Indeed, to those engaged in movements for the liberation from colonial rule the truth must sometimes have seemed closer to the opposite: to them it was the British (or the French or the Dutch) who appeared to be on the side of inequality, and the Indians (or the Indo-Chinese or the Indonesians) on the side of equality. These experiences cannot be easily set aside as mere surface phenomena, representing a particular moment in history: colonialism has been a fairly long moment in modern history.

As one might expect, the case for a consistently hierarchical normative order rests not so much on the experience of modern India as on an image of India's past. The modern Constitution of India, with its project of a 'casteless and classless society', is ignored, while the *Manusmriti* with its concern for the order of *varnas* is shown as providing a kind of timeless charter for Indian society. To say that the modern Constitution, with its strong emphasis on equality, is of foreign inspiration would be to assert a half truth. It would be to ignore the fact that its writing was the culmination of a historical process in which Indians looked to other lands as well as their own past in order to give themselves a clear conception of equality. It is an essential point in my argument that when in this quest they turned to their own past, they did not find a complete void; and it is this point that is thoroughly obscured by the thesis about *homo hierarchicus.*

And the thesis about *homo equalis* falsifies the history of colonial rule. The modern West's most dramatic denial of equality—not just the practice of equality, but the principle—was not at home but in the colonies. And so, again not unexpectedly, the colonial context is kept discreetly in the background in the many facile expositions that celebrate the triumph of egalitarianism in the West.

Despite their surface appeal, the more deeply we examine them, the more it appears that *homo hierarchicus* as well as *homo equalis* are paste-board characters. Perhaps such characters have a certain pedagogical function in so far as they make quick and sharp contrasts possible between societies widely separated in space and time. But a major civilization, such as the Indian or the Western, is too rich and too complex to be adequately portrayed by the one to the exclusion of the other. Such portrayal tends above all to sacrifice history and the interplay between principle and practice by fixing attention on what are believed to be unchanging structures.

The thesis about *homo hierarchicus* has thus another implication as well. This is that *homo hierarchicus* is not only single-minded in his attachment to inequality but also deeply resistant to change. The thesis first attributes to certain societies a hierarchical structure, and then denies them all internal resources for creating or sustaining institutions based on the principle of equality. Thus it is argued that democratic institutions are foreign plants on the Indian soil and, being foreign plants, they are bound to wither or sicken. By this kind of theory the reasons for the collapse of democracy in India between 1975 and 1977 are in principle, and not by any test of historical evidence, different from the reasons for its collapse in Germany between 1934 and 1945. When democracy fails in the land of *homo hierarchicus* it does so by the logic of an unchanging structure; when it fails in the land of *homo equalis* it does so by reason of particular historical circumstance.

Equality and inequality are both of them large ideas, so rich and inexhaustible in their meanings that it seems strange to think that any society, let alone a major civilization, should have failed to dwell on the significance of each of them for man's relations to his fellow men. It is not in the absence of the one or the other that we should expect to find the specificities of a civilization, but in the manner in which the two are conceived and related to each other in the light of historical experience. To argue that each civilization has its own design is surely not to say that that design can be made intelligible by a simple formula.

Ideas of equality and inequality are in all societies built into conceptions of justice, and no society exists without a conception of justice. The conception of justice rarely, if ever, rests solely on a simple arithmetical notion of equality in which all the constituent parts of a society, whether individuals or classes, are equally regarded in every respect. What is far more common is the attempt, needless to say only in principle, to establish equality by bringing about a just proportion between reward and merit. It is an old argument, and one probably acknowledged by every civilization, ancient as well as modern, that the ends of justice are defeated when equals are treated unequally, but also when unequals are treated equally.

Some philosophers have maintained against egalitarians that all that they are able to argue for is the equal consideration of human worth, and that this leaves us in the end with a kind of residual idea of equality. But even this is important if only because it shows how difficult it is to formulate a principle of justice without some consideration for equality, however residual. For justice requires that consideration be given to human beings as human beings, to what they have in common, and not merely to the myriad differences that no doubt exist among them. And if justice so conceived is denied by the king's law, there are above it the laws of God, or of nature, or of history. I find it difficult to believe that the idea of human beings as equal claimants to justice in this broad sense can be a monopoly of any one society or culture to the exclusion of all others.

At the same time, it is difficult to conceive of a society in which no discrimination is made in this world among human beings according to merit, quality or worth. Evaluation is, clearly, a universal feature of human culture, and evaluation and discrimination are only two sides of the same coin. Every society creates its own conception of merit, and constructs its own devices for ensuring that merit receives its due recognition and reward. Again, the fact that there always is disagreement over what is due in the particular case does not mean that the principle itself is denied or ignored.

One might argue no doubt that some societies apply discrimination rationally while others do so arbitrarily; or, in other words, that only some societies have discovered what true merit is, and are able to give it its due reward, whereas others either are unable to recognize merit or take little or no account of it in allocating rewards. The contrast between *homo hierarchicus* and *homo equalis* very often conceals some such unstated argument. *Homo hierarchicus* not only discriminates compulsively between superior and inferior, but generally does so on quixotic grounds. *Homo equalis* is loath to discriminate, except that without discrimination merit would wither in the bloom.

A parallel argument is that inequalities are small or of peripheral significance in some societies whereas in others they are large or of central significance. Or, that in some societies inequalities exist within a basic framework of equality whereas in others the reverse holds true. T. H. Marshall maintained that contemporary Western societies were governed by a principle of 'qualitative equality' which, to be sure, was capable of accommodating 'quantitative inequality' in such matters as income and expenditure.[1] This is not altogether different from the argument of contemporary Soviet sociologists that, while there are classes in Soviet society, the distinctions among them are 'non-basic' in contrast to the 'basic' distinctions that exist among classes in capitalist societies.[2]

The problem is that, though plausible to an extent when considered by themselves, these arguments look rather thin when confronted with each other. Soviet sociologists would no doubt regard the contrast made by Marshall between 'qualitative equality' and 'quantitative inequality' as a mere play on words, for, according to their theory or ideology, the inequalities between classes in capitalist society are basic, fundamental and qualitative. The Chinese do not appear to encourage the profession of sociology, but if they did, their sociologists would in turn view with similar scepticism the Soviet claim that they have replaced 'basic' class distinctions by 'non-basic' ones.

Societies differ greatly from each other in their morphology, as even a casual comparison between China and the Soviet Union, or between the Soviet Union and the United States will reveal. They

[1] T. H. Marshall, *Sociology at the Crossroads and Other Essays*, Heinemann, 1963, p. 72.

[2] See, for instance, G. Glezerman, *Socialist Society*, Progress Publishers, 1971, p. 106.

also differ in their ideology, although today they vie with each other in proclaiming their adherence to equality. Each of these societies— China, the Soviet Union, the United States—is the product of a social revolution which placed the principle of equality at its centre, and each has impressive achievements to its credit. And yet one wonders if any of them has succeeded in finally laying the ghost of inequality.

And what about the ghost of equality in the so-called hierarchical societies of the past? India is taken as a text-book example of a hierarchical society, but, despite the impressive body of evidence about the durability of caste—whether as *varna* or as *jati*—it would be difficult to maintain that even in India there ever was a complete rejection or denial of equality as a value and an ideal. The burden of caste, with its oppressive gradations, generated its own antithesis on the ideological plane, and the question of equality was insistently raised in a succession of religious movements that go back to the beginnings of recorded history.

For these reasons I find it false to represent the opposition between equality and inequality as a contrast between two societies in two different parts of the world. On the contrary, each society is an arena within which the two interplay, and if we fail to examine this inter-play within societies, the comparisons we make between societies will be shallow and misleading. We can talk about *homo hierarchicus* and *homo equalis* only if we recognize that there is something of both in every human society and perhaps in every human individual.

The contrast between hierarchical and egalitarian societies is not a new one. It is a contrast that has been repeatedly made by students of the history of Western societies within the context of their own civilization. In the period following the French Revolution it was common to contrast the fixed and stable hierarchies of the old regime with the fluid and open arrangements of the new society. The contrast was not confined to the legal order alone, but extended to every aspect of society and culture, from politics to art. Those who first drew attention to the contrast were witnessing the replacement of one social order by another, and it is not surprising that they dwelt as much on the rigidity of the one as on the flexibility of the other.

The contrast comes up retrospectively when students of stratification in contemporary Western societies seek to delineate the contours of the social pyramid in their own time. Sociologists are notorious for their failure to agree on the nature and number of classes or strata in the societies in which they live. Their failure leads some of them to look back nostalgically to their own past when, presumably, there was a wide and general agreement about the prevailing hierarchy which, according to the argument, was coterminous with the social order as such.

Among the most celebrated of such contrasts between the old order of Western society and the new is the one we owe to Alexis de Tocqueville. For Tocqueville there were two kinds of societies, aristocratic society with its fixed and stable hierarchy of estates or castes, and democratic society which allowed or even encouraged the free movement of individuals across its classes. Aristocratic societies prevailed in Europe prior to the nineteenth century; and America in the first half of that century was the best example of democratic society. In his own day France with its 'half-ruined scale of classes' was seeking uneasily to move from one type of social order to the other.[3]

As Tocqueville saw aristocratic societies, they were characterized not only by a particular morphology but also by a particular mentality or state of mind. The morphology and the mentality reinforced each other. Morphologically there was a division of society into castes or estates with well-defined boundaries between them. The individual had no recognizable identity of his own, but took his identity from the caste or estate to which he belonged. Relations between individuals were governed not by free choice, but by their respective positions in the hierarchical order of society.

Tocqueville's work brings out the ambiguities in the relations between the different layers in a hierarchical society. On the one hand, there is the feeling that these layers constitute different worlds, separated from each other by beliefs, manners and sentiments. 'Among an aristocratic people each caste has its own opinions, feelings, rights, customs, and modes of living. Thus the men who compose it do not resemble the mass of their fellow citizens; they do not think or feel in the same manner, and they scarcely believe that they belong to the same race.'[4] On the other hand, there are close, even intimate, personal ties running up and down the various layers of the hierarchy. For, 'As in aristocratic communities all the citizens

[3] A. de Tocqueville, *Democracy in America*, Alfred Knopf, 1956, vol. 2, p. 173.
[4] Ibid., vol. 2, p. 163.

4

occupy fixed positions, one above another, the result is that each of
them always sees a man above himself whose patronage is necessary
to him, and below himself another man whose co-operation he may
claim.'[5]

The nature of an aristocratic society is revealed in the relations
between masters and servants, between landlords and tenants, between men and women, and between the generations. In an aristocracy there are not only masters and servants, but servants develop
their own hierarchy which reproduces the hierarchy of their masters.
The master sees the servant as a secondary or inferior part of himself, and the servant seeks to efface his own identity in that of his
master. In this way the hierarchy is perpetuated, being accepted as a
part of the natural scheme of things by inferiors as well as superiors.

In an aristocracy every organ of society mirrors the hierarchy of
the larger social organism. The family no less than the kingdom or
nation has its hierarchy. Men and women are unequally placed.
There is a strict order of precedence between the generations, and,
within each generation, between senior and junior members. Each
family is a link not only between the various layers of society, but
also between past and future generations. In Tocqueville's words,
'Among aristocratic nations, as families remain for centuries in the
same condition, often on the same spot, all generations become, as it
were, contemporaneous. A man almost always knows his forefathers
and respects them; he thinks he already sees his remote descendants
and he loves them.'[6] In other words, hierarchy and stability are in-
timately linked.

What Tocqueville seems to be saying is that the distinctive feature
of an aristocratic society lies not simply in the existence of inequalities
of condition but in the fact that the same people, or people from the
same families, fill the same ranks in society from generation to
generation. He does speak of an aristocracy of wealth which he
contrasts with an aristocracy of birth; and of a business or industrial
aristocracy which he contrasts with a landed or territorial aristocracy. But for him, an aristocracy in the true sense of the term was
always one based on birth and rooted in the soil.

Democratic societies are radically different in constitution from
aristocratic ones. They are based on the principle of equality which
permeates every area of human existence. Tocqueville did not give a
precise or single meaning to the term equality. Rather, he dwelt on

its various aspects and forms in order to build up a picture of democratic society which made it appear to be the very opposite of aristocratic society. In customs, morals, religion and politics a democracy is the opposite of an aristocracy, and the difference is in each case due to the presence or absence of equality.

Tocqueville attached great importance to the equality of conditions, meaning generally the conditions of material existence. His conception of a democratic society was above all of one in which there would not be extremes of either wealth or poverty. He was typical of his times in being unable to conceive of vast fortunes in trade or industry on a scale at all comparable to the vast fortunes that had been common among the landed aristocracy. Nor was he much struck by that aspect of industrial life which was to fix the attention of Marx and Engels a short while after: the misery and squalor of the industrial slum.

Tocqueville attributed the lack of extremes to the fact that neither wealth nor poverty was cumulative within the family. Inequalities were bound to be small because there were no fixed orders in a democratic society to prevent the losses suffered in one generation from being made good by gains achieved in the next. Because the boundaries between the strata were so fluid, their very character was different from the character of those in an aristocratic society. Indeed, in Tocqueville's scheme these strata have a residual character in a democratic society which is, in this sense, a complex of individuals rather than a hierarchy of estates.

For Tocqueville equality was not merely a matter of external conditions in democratic society, it was a way of life. He recognized that the external conditions of life could never be fully equalized. But inequalities in these conditions had been substantially reduced, and would be further reduced; moreover, what remained would count for little since men's attitudes will have been radically transformed. While there might still be masters and servants in a democracy, there would be a basic equality between them as their relations became increasingly contractual.

The attraction of Tocqueville's work lies in his refusal to be a prisoner of his own dichotomy. While he dwells at great length on the opposite natures of aristocratic and democratic societies, he leaves room for considering the contradictions within each type of society.

It is clear that equality as an ideal and a value was never wholly alien to Western civilization even when its organization was most elaborately hierarchical. No institution within that civilization was more hierarchical than the Catholic church, and indeed the concept of hierarchy is in its deepest meaning a Christian concept. Tocqueville recognized and noted this; at the same time he did not fail to point out that 'Christianity, which has declared that all men are equal in the sight of God, will not refuse to acknowledge that all citizens are equal in the eye of the law'.[7] It is as if a value and an ideal that had lain dormant under a hierarchical organization came into its own when external conditions favoured its awakening, and then invested these external conditions with a new significance.

Tocqueville drew attention repeatedly to the particular combination of external conditions that favoured the growth of democracy in America. But even in America the fabric of democracy was flawed by the cleavages of race. In a land devoted to the pursuit of equality there was no equality among the races, and American society was, if anything, a multiracial society. Tocqueville believed that the three principal races of America were unequally endowed by nature in ability and talent; and his advocacy extended to the abolition of only the privileges established by law, not of those established by nature. Even so, the destruction of the Indians and the enslavement of the Blacks—so vividly portrayed by Tocqueville himself—could hardly have left the commitment to equality unaffected among the pioneers of democracy in America.

Tocqueville was not alone in viewing pre-capitalist European society as a hierarchy. This view of it was widely held, although some might argue that the hierarchy merely concealed the deeper contradictions inherent in real life. Marx and Engels wrote in *The German Ideology*, 'Hierarchy is the ideal form of feudalism; feudalism is the political form of the medieval relations of production and commerce.'[8] This appears to offer a better balanced picture by inviting us to consider not merely the hierarchy but also what the hierarchy concealed.

The dramatic force of the opposition between hierarchy and equality is greatly enhanced when two different civilizations are

[7] Ibid., vol. 1, p. 12.

[8] K. Marx and F. Engels, *The German Ideology*, Progress Publishers, 1968, p. 190.

contrasted instead of two phases in the development of the same civilization. The contrast between medieval and modern Europe came thus to be gradually displaced by a contrast between the East and the West. By the end of the nineteenth century this contrast began to present itself in a variety of forms: the everchanging West as opposed to the unchanging East; Eastern religiosity as opposed to Western materialism; the democratic West as opposed to the despotic or the hierarchical East. The fact that the forms of the contrast were not always mutually consistent did not reduce the force of the contrast. So pervasive was the contrast that it is difficult to escape the suspicion that it fulfilled some purpose in the relations among nations.

However much one might contrast one's own past with one's present, it becomes difficult beyond a point to fix the character of this past in terms of one unique principle. The more closely one examines the old order in the West the less plausible the argument appears that it knew nothing of equality as a value. The encounter with historical evidence—unavoidable in the study of one's own society—tends to subdue the contrast between the old order of hierarchy and the new order of equality. Also, the need to relate the present to the past leads to a more differentiated view of the one as well as the other.

It is far easier to accept an undifferentiated view of an alien society. In one's own society there is continuity as well as change: the threads run clearly between the past and the present. Other societies are not only different, they are always different in the same way. To look at one society as a historical entity and the other in ahistorical terms is to vitiate the comparison between them. The task of comparison, on the other hand, is not to decide once and for all whether societies are basically the same or basically different, but to reveal differences where sameness was assumed and sameness where difference was taken for granted.

A common Western characterization of Asian societies is that they are despotic. The emphasis here is on the oppressive machinery of state and, more generally, on inequalities in the distribution of power. Examples of such societies are chosen from all over Asia, ranging from Turkey through Iran and India to China. In the writings of some the category 'Asiatic' or 'Oriental' is used very widely to include, in addition, societies from both Africa and pre-Columbian America. In the extreme case virtually all forms of state organization other than the democracies of the West may be characterized as despotic.

Explanations of the inequalities of power in the Oriental state have been sought in a particular mode of production, the so-called Asiatic mode of production. According to the theory, this mode of production generated its own apparatus of coercion which in its turn permeated every sphere of society and culture. There is still controversy as to the place that the Asiatic mode of production occupies in the Marxian scheme of analysis. Marx's own writings would seem to indicate that he shared in the prevalent Western view regarding China and India, that they were at the same time despotic and hierarchical.

The most vigorous recent presentation of the argument about Oriental despotism is to be found in Karl Wittfogel's comparative study of the subject published a little over twenty years ago.[9] The study claims to examine the 'institutional settings' of Oriental despotism and, although the most detailed treatment is reserved for China, there is a fairly extended discussion of India as well. Wittfogel's work is animated by his antipathy to modern totalitarian regimes. These, according to him, find their most congenial institutional settings in Asiatic societies to which the ideals of democracy and the norms of equality are alien. Those whom he claims as having provided inspiration for his ideas include James Mill as well as Karl Marx.

For what he says about ancient India, Wittfogel relies primarily on two well-known classical texts, the *Arthashastra* of Kautilya and the *Dharmashastra* of Manu. By a judicious selection of quotations he is able to show how the masses were kept in total subordination through the use of arbitrary power by the king and his numerous agents. The *Arthashastra* is quoted to show what an elaborate apparatus of officials and spies was required to ensure the smooth functioning of the system. And, finally, according to Wittfogel, 'The Hindu law book of Manu established fear-inspiring punishment as the foundation of internal peace and order.'[10]

Inequality has more than one form, and Wittfogel's emphasis throughout is on inequalities of power—the gulf in Asiatic societies between the ruler and his apparatus on the one hand, and the common people on the other. Also, his preoccupation with total power

[9] K. Wittfogel, *Oriental Despotism: A Comparative Study of Total Power*, Yale University Press, 1957.   [10] Ibid., p. 138.

leads him to contrast the apparatus with the people, without his paying too much attention to the hierarchical chain of command and obedience. At the same time, he indicates the far-reaching implications of a machinery of total power for the entire range of social relations. Thus, he discusses how societies governed by total power develop their own peculiar symbols of superordination and subordination and how, more generally, the apparatus of state uses religion to serve its own ends.

Not everyone has sought the root of inequality in traditional India in its political order. Indeed, the more common practice has been to seek it in the realm of religion, particularly Hinduism. Recently Louis Dumont has published an impressive account of the caste system in India.[11] Dumont's work has captured the imagination of a large number of social scientists by the boldness of its contrast between traditional India and the modern West. Dumont's theoretical orientation differs sharply from Wittfogel's in so far as he takes pains to assign a subordinate position to the politico-economic order in India. Thus, whereas Wittfogel's concern is with despotism, Dumont's is with hierarchy; whereas Wittfogel speaks of totalitarianism, Dumont speaks of holism. One might occasionally wonder, though, whether holism might not be merely the ideal form of totalitarianism.

Dumont constructs a picture of an elaborate hierarchy of castes in which each individual is kept in his place not by means of punishment or the arbitrary exercise of power, but through the universal acceptance of the values of a hierarchical order. In a hierarchical order the Untouchable no less than the Brahmin accepts his allotted place, because thoughts of equality do not disturb their minds. It appears to me that Dumont's originality lies less in the substance of his argument than in the uncompromising manner of its presentation.

Despite its categorical tone, Dumont's argument is in fact complex. Firstly, there are two oppositions: between hierarchy and equality, and between holism and individualism. The relationship between the two oppositions is not absolutely clear. In his earlier work on India the emphasis was on hierarchy and holism or, rather, on hierarchy as an aspect of holism. In his more recent work on Europe the emphasis seems to be more on individualism than on equality. Although Dumont seems prepared to concede the possibility of a

[11] L. Dumont, *Homo Hierarchicus: The Caste System and Its Implications*, Paladin, 1972.

combination of holism and equality—as in the case of Islam—in what he has to say about the West, the argument is maintained that individualism entails equality.

Secondly, the societies being compared are not two but three. There is, most prominently, the contrast between hierarchy in India and equality in the West, but there is also the contrast between the old and the new orders of Western society. The point of departure of *Homo Hierarchicus* is Tocqueville's work. Tocqueville's contrast between aristocracy and democracy is reformulated as a contrast between hierarchy and equality. Dumont makes it quite plain that there was a historical break in Western society which led to the replacement of holism and hierarchy by individualism and equality. He follows Tocqueville very closely here in asserting that individualism—and its counterpart equality—is a modern phenomenon in the West.

The initial contrast is between modern society and traditional societies. According to this contrast, 'As opposed to modern society traditional societies . . . know nothing of equality and liberty as values . . . know nothing, in short, of the individual. . . .'[12] Or, a little further on, 'It is striking to find out how recent and belated is the development of the idea of equality and its implications. In the eighteenth century it played only a secondary role, except in the works of Helvetius and Morelly.'[13] Thus, while talking about traditional societies Dumont has in mind not merely traditional India but also the *ancien régime* of the West. Indeed, the argument is taken directly from Tocqueville, although the tone is typically Dumont's: it would be unusual for Tocqueville to assert that aristocratic societies knew *nothing* of 'equality and liberty as values'.

Having served its purpose in introducing the argument, traditional society in the West disappears from view in the rest of Dumont's discussion in *Homo Hierarchicus*. At the end of a detailed analysis of the ritual hierarchy of the Hindus, the concluding chapter presents a contrast between hierarchical and egalitarian societies; but here the contrast is no longer between 'traditional' and 'modern' societies, but between India and the West. One is left wondering why the contrast with which the argument began, between the old and the new orders of Western society—Tocqueville's contrast—is never taken up again at the end.

If the main contrast is between holism and individualism, or

[12] Ibid., p. 42.   [13] Ibid., p. 46.

between hierarchy and equality, one naturally asks where the traditional West stands in Dumont's scheme: with India (which clearly
exemplifies holism and hierarchy) or with the modern West (which
equally clearly exemplifies individualism and equality)? Dumont
appears to fight shy of a clear answer here. For the more closely he
examines the Western past, the less sharp appears its contrast with
the Western present. In his recent study of ideology in the West we
are told that 'individualism was a characteristic of Christian thought
from the start';[14] a rather far cry from the assertion in *Homo Hierarchicus* that traditional societies know *nothing* of the individual.
Having come so far, it would be but a short step to the point that
equality and liberty as well were characteristics of Christian thought
from the start; an argument not out of tune with the spirit of Tocqueville.

Dumont is obliged to soften his contrast between the old and the
new orders in the West by his concern for Western history. But there
is no comparable concern for Indian history that might show that
the Indian tradition also is neither undifferentiated nor unchanging.
History is indispensable in understanding the West, but it can be
dispensed with in understanding India, since all phases of Indian
history are dominated by the same unchanging structure. It is thus
that the contrast between the *modern* West and *traditional* India is
reduced to a simple contrast between India and the West.

One would like to see a serious comparison made between the
traditional West and traditional India. Was Tocqueville merely using
a metaphor when he spoke of castes in the old order of European
society? If, as Marx and Engels said, hierarchy was the ideal form
of feudalism, how did this hierarchy differ from the one represented
in the Hindu *Dharmashastras*? What should also be considered,
along with the recognition of the hierarchy in the legal order, is its
frequent repudiation in moral discourse in Western as well as Eastern
religions.

Above all, we must consider modern India along with the modern
West since the historical forces that created the one are closely
intermeshed with those that created the other. Although Dumont's
case for holism and hierarchy in India rests in large part on ethnographic data collected during the last couple of decades, he fails to
consider the distinctive historical forces that have shaped modern

[14] L. Dumont, *From Mandeville to Marx: The Genesis and Triumph of Economic
Ideology*, University of Chicago Press, 1977, p. 15.

as opposed to traditional India. Dumont dismisses the argument that there has been any significant change in the structure of Indian society. In any case, he points out, structures do not change, they are either present or absent; and there is no clear evidence of a new structure, although cracks might have appeared in the old. All things considered, it is a little strange that an anthropologist who is able to see the past so clearly should find the present so puzzling.

More recently Dumont has argued that holism (and presumably also hierarchy) is a feature not only of India but also of China and Japan. In his own words, 'There is no doubt that traditional Chinese, Japanese and Indian ideologies are holistic while ours is individualistic.'[15] This, surely, is reminiscent of Wittfogel in its sweep. It may be that with most practitioners of the craft the real as opposed to the stated objective of comparative sociology is to demonstrate the uniqueness of Western civilization. Other civilizations are then sketched out as a painter might sketch out a background, to bring out with better effect what lies on the foreground. Treating other civilizations in this way does violence to their history and their living character.

In the nineteenth century the established hierarchy of caste and the ideology by which it was supported came under severe attack as a result of India's exposure to the West. This exposure created a new consciousness and new attitudes to equality and inequality that were different from what had prevailed until then in India as well as in the West. Contemporary Indian attitudes differ from the attitudes of nineteenth century Indians in regard to caste. But they differ also from nineteenth century Western attitudes in regard to race; Tocqueville was not what we might call a racist, but his views on the races of mankind are not likely to pass unchallenged in India today.

I am not trying to suggest that the modern Indian has an unwavering commitment to equality, whether among castes or among races, for I do not believe that human beings by and large have such an unwavering commitment anywhere. Rather, the intelligentsia that helped to shape the values of modern India found itself in a peculiar historical predicament in the nineteenth century. It was essentially an upper caste intelligentsia which had within its traditional cultural

---

[15] Ibid., p. 9.

context taken its own social superiority for granted. It now found itself despised, and its traditional culture denigrated by alien rulers acutely conscious of their own racial superiority. The situation itself called for an assertion of equality as a general value, not merely equality among races or among nations, but also equality among castes and among human beings in general.

There is no doubt that Indians in the nineteenth century learnt a great deal about equality from their encounter with the West. The point that I am trying to make is that they probably learnt more about it from the Western practice of inequality than from the Western theory of equality. Above all, they were led to reflect on their own society and its past by the injury done to them by alien rulers whom they both admired and hated.

Thus, the preoccupation with equality that is a feature of the Constitution of India figures as an important theme in the intellectual debates of nineteenth century India. A striking expression of this preoccupation is to be found in the works of the nineteenth century Bengali writer Bankimchandra Chatterji whose literary activities covered a wide range and exercised a considerable influence. Bankim, who represents what may be called a conservative point of view, was greatly influenced by both traditional Sanskritic learning and modern western scientific and historical knowledge. In 1879, he published a tract on Equality,[16] and, although it was later repudiated by him, it shows a concern for the problem that is authentic and deeply felt.

For most of his active life Bankim served the British as a middle-level civil servant in the districts of Bengal. A man of his intellect and learning must have often been irked by the high-handedness of his official superiors who were generally British and not always inspiring, and this pique is expressed in some of the sketches that he wrote at the time. In his tract on Equality Bankim deals with discrimination against the poor by the rich, against Shudras by Brahmans, and against women by men, but it is perhaps no accident that he begins with an attack on the symbols of office, symbols which had a luxuriant growth under colonial rule in every part of the world.

What was distinctive of this consciousness was that it led to a reappraisal of old inequalities in the light of new ones. Bankim addressed himself to his fellow Indians smarting under the humiliation of colonial rule, and asked them why they should complain

[16] Bankimchandra Chatterji, *Bankim Rachanabali* (in Bengali), Sahitya Samsad, 1382 (Bengali calendar), vol. II, pp. 381–406.

about the inequality of races when they had been quite happy to accept the inequality of castes. Though a conservative who claimed to be wholly committed to the spirit of Hinduism, Bankim was relentless in his exposure of the many inequalities institutionalized within Hindu society. It was a popular argument among Indians in his time that the oppression of inferior by superior *varnas* was less harsh than the oppression of the Indians by the British since all *varnas* were of the same race. Bankim rejected this argument on the ground that to the oppressed it mattered little whether their oppressors were of the same or another race.[17]

The argument that there is little to choose between the inequalities of caste and race has implications for inequalities of every kind. These implications began to surface with every major step taken by Indians towards emancipation from colonial rule. The demand for an end to colonial rule could hardly be made effective without a demand for the reconstitution of Indian society.

Bankim's essay on Equality discusses the contradiction between principle and practice, and argues that human societies decay and degenerate whenever they become set in a rigidly hierarchical mould. A new spirit has then to be kindled in these societies so that they acquire a new lease of life. Bankim speaks of three prophets of equality who have revitalized human societies in this way. The last of these, according to him, was Rousseau.

The appeal to Rousseau did not signify a lack of faith in the resources of traditional Indian culture. Indeed, India's present was contrasted with her past, her social institutions with her values and ideals. Bankim argued that however debased these institutions might be, they never succeeded in fully effacing certain fundamental human values. And Rousseau was for him only the last and the least perfect of the prophets of equality, the first among whom was the Buddha.

Indians who have felt oppressed by the burden of caste have naturally been reluctant to concede that caste represented the sum total or even the essence of their tradition. To view this tradition as a storehouse of complex and conflicting values is, surely, not to deny the place of caste or hierarchy in it. Nor is it historically true that antipathy to the hierarchy of caste was never quickened among Indians before they became exposed to the egalitarian ideals of the West. Indeed the response to these ideals could hardly be what it was if they raised no echoes at all within the Indian tradition itself.

[17] Ibid., pp. 241–5.

Some of the most influential thinkers of modern India have condemned the hierarchy of caste and at the same time expressed their
commitment to what they considered to be the fundamental values of
Indian society. Two outstanding examples among the makers of
modern India were Rabindranath Tagore and Mahatma Gandhi who
both condemned the institution of caste and argued that equality
was a fundamental value within the Indian tradition. I am not suggesting that arguments about a society's past are established simply
because they appeal to millions of its people in the present. But I do
believe that such arguments have to be seriously considered in a
study of ideologies; and they have not been considered by those who
assert that Indian society was hierarchical to the point that ideas of
equality were wholly excluded from it.

As a member of the Brahmo Samaj which had broken away from
orthodox Hinduism, Tagore was a severe critic of caste in general
and untouchability in particular. Unlike other Brahmos, Tagore
continued to regard himself as a Hindu and drew copiously from the
Hindu tradition in what he wrote. Again, he did not deny the
significance of caste in India's historical development; rather, he
maintained that the basic spirit of Indian culture itself required that
caste be condemned. He too turned to Buddhism as a perennial
source of inspiration for egalitarian values and symbols.

Gandhi was much more actively involved in the reconstruction of
Hindu society than Tagore. He was also much more firmly rooted
in the Hindu religious tradition. He saw himself as a religious man,
and was seen as such by millions of Indians. Gandhi was one of the
great exemplars of equality in modern times, and it would be strange
to argue that his commitment to equality was wholly Western in
inspiration.

Gandhi used the treatment of Untouchables by the upper castes
as a symbol of caste discrimination, and he attacked it strongly in
words as well as deeds. His campaign against untouchability led him
to write extensively about the place of caste in the Hindu scheme of
things. These writings appeared regularly in his paper *Harijan* which
was the name he had coined for the Untouchables.

Gandhi's writings on *varna, jati*, untouchability, equality and inequality are always forceful, but not without ambiguity. He made a
sharp distinction between *varna*, which he endorsed, and *jati* or
caste, which he condemned. He maintained that as a Hindu he was
committed to *varna* which, in principle, represented a division of

functions, and had nothing to do with superiority and inferiority. The proliferation of *jatis*, with their myriad forms of discrimination, was, according to Gandhi, contrary to the spirit of Hinduism.

Gandhi was aware that the Hindu *Dharmashastras* sanctioned the hierarchical ranking of castes. Indeed, this was often pointed out to him by the orthodox defenders of the caste system in India. But against this Gandhi maintained that the *Dharmashastras* did not represent the ultimate truth of Hinduism. This truth, according to him, was represented by the *Gita* which viewed the relationship between man and man in another light. Gandhi maintained that where there was divergence between the *Gita* and the *Dharmashastras*, it was the duty of every Hindu to be guided by the former; and that he himself would renounce Hinduism if it could be proved that the *Gita* sanctioned inequality among castes.[18]

I find it difficult to decide whether the *Gita* is more authoritative or the *Dharmashastras*. But I do hope that the issues I have raised show that the Hindu is a somewhat more complex animal than the simple view of him as *homo hierarchicus* would make him out to be. The *Dharmashastras* undoubtedly tell us much about the institutional order of Hinduism. But there is a whole tradition of moral discourse from the *Mahabharata* down to modern times which is animated by a different spirit from that of the *Dharmashastras*. It would be rash to ignore this tradition, particularly where the objective is to represent not merely the institutions of a society but its ultimate values.

The argument that Indian society is unalterably hierarchical was built up during the high tide of imperial rule. It was not built up in a day, and a great deal of scholarship went into it. Both Indians and Europeans contributed to this scholarship, and in some ways the Indians themselves became the most bitter critics of the hierarchical aspects of caste. But within the imperialist order the argument had also a political function which it would be disingenuous to overlook: to assert that Indians are unalterably hierarchical is also to maintain that in the modern world they are less than fit for self-governance.

The contrast between *homo hierarchicus* and *homo equalis* in the specific historical form in which it was presented was hardly likely to appeal in the same way to the victims and the beneficiaries of imperial rule. Those who trace the historical conditions of the emergence of *homo equalis* in the West generally overlook the adventures

18 M. K. Gandhi, *Varnashramadharma*, Navjivan Publishing House, 1962.

of the same *homo equalis* abroad. As if the destruction of aboriginal society in Australia and America, the enslavement and brutal use of millions of Blacks, or the imposition of the most unequal conditions between Europeans and natives throughout Asia took place in another epoch or on a different planet.

It would be naive to argue that imperialism was merely a matter of power, that it did not create its own ideology, its own values and its own symbols. Surely, in the early years of this century the hierarchical symbols of the British Raj in India were just as extravagant as those of caste. And hierarchical values permeated every kind of relationship between Whites and natives in the Third World. It is difficult to believe that all of this affected *homo equalis* only abroad and left him completely unaffected at home. It is this other face of *homo equalis*, both at home and abroad, that was so vividly portrayed by George Orwell in his early work.[19]

While serving a term in a British jail in India, Nehru wrote, 'The spirit of the age is in favour of equality, though practice denies it almost everywhere.'[20] I like to believe that Nehru had in mind not only his fellow Indians who courted imprisonment in the name of equality and at the same time practised untouchability, but also the British who proclaimed the virtues of democracy even while advocating the necessity of imperialism. I find that Nehru's formulation provides a far more insightful approach to the structure of the modern world than a black-and-white contrast between *homo hierarchicus* and *homo equalis*. That kind of contrast falsifies history, and can lead in the end only to self-congratulation.

[19] In particular, *Burmese Days* and *The Road to Wigan Pier*.
[20] J. Nehru, *The Discovery of India*, Asia Publishing House, 1961, p. 521.

Harmonic and Disharmonic Social Systems

Lecture delivered at the University of Sydney,
1971/1982

I would like to examine in this lecture in the general context of in-equality the distinction between two kinds of social system which I describe as 'harmonic' and 'disharmonic' social systems. A harmonic system is one in which there is consistency between the normative order and the existential order: society is divided into groups which are placed high and low, and the divisions and their ordering are con-sidered as right, proper and desirable or as a part of the natural scheme of things. A disharmonic system by constrast shows a lack of consistency between the existential and the normative orders: the norm of equality is contradicted by the pervasive existence of in-equality. Following this terminology, one might describe as 'har-monic' a system in which there is equality in both principle and practice, and as 'disharmonic' one in which people practise equality while professing its opposite; but these I exclude from consideration as being remote from historical experience.

I recognize that the distinction between harmonic and disharmonic systems has to be applied with utmost caution to actual social and historical reality which is by its very nature resistant to neat contrasts and clear-cut distinctions. At the same time, it is an illuminating distinction to the extent that it throws into sharp relief an outstanding characteristic of the contemporary world which is the contradiction between the ideal of equality and the experience of inequality.

The contradiction between the ideal of equality and the experience of inequality has become a commonplace of contemporary debate and discussion. Constitutions, laws and public statements of every kind in the modern world lean heavily on the side of equality. The case for equality is taken for granted and where it has to be made it is made firmly and openly. Inequality, on the other hand, is not defended for its own sake but in the interest of some other value, e.g.

liberty or efficiency. At the same time, inequality not only between individuals but also between collectivities, such as races or nations, is a pervasive feature of contemporary existence.

Is the contradiction between ideal and reality known only to the contemporary world? It would clearly be hazardous to maintain about any social system that there is perfect consistency between its various parts or aspects. Such a system would have no room in it at all for conflict or for change. Societies remote from our own in either space or time present an appearance of stability and harmony that is to some extent illusory. The distinction between harmonic and disharmonic social systems rests at least in part on the difference of perspective to which we are doomed in comparing the past with the present.

The contrast between harmonic and disharmonic systems, as I make it, seeks to bring together the two basic concerns of sociology, the study of facts and of values, or of existence and consciousness, or of the material and the ideal. This way of dividing up social reality or the subject matter of sociology is not free from serious difficulty. To take a very familiar example, when we talk about the relationship between social existence and social consciousness, are we talking about a relationship between two parts on the same plane or about a relationship between a whole and one of its parts? And, if the latter, which is the whole and which is the part?[1]

The plain fact is that what we call social existence is not something palpable or tangible and, while it may have some of the characteristics of material reality, it can be apprehended only partially as such. It is for this reason that Durkheim's famous dictum to consider social facts as things has to be applied with caution. For, as it has rightly been pointed out, if social facts are things, they are also representations.[2] However, it would be an impermissible step from this to contend that social reality has no existence beyond the ideas of it people carry in their heads.

It is to Durkheim that we owe the first systematic attempt at a

[1] The distinction, which is in some sense the pivot of Marx's sociology, between social being and social consciousness, bristles with difficulty. There are various orthodox versions of the distinction by Marxists from Plekhanov to Lukacs. I have discussed the problem briefly in my M. N. Roy Memorial lecture. See André Béteille, *Marxism, Pluralism and Orthodoxy*, Indian Renaissance Institute (New Delhi), 1982.

[2] Claude Lévi-Strauss, 'French Sociology' in Georges Gurvitch and Wilbert E. Moore, *Twentieth-Century Sociology*, The Philosophical Library, 1945, pp. 503–37.

morphological approach to the understanding of human societies.[3] This approach defines social structure in terms of the enduring groups in a society, their arrangement and their relationships. It views inequality in terms of an external framework fixed by the division of society into groups and their placement in a certain order of ranks. An order of estates or of castes has an existence that is in some sense independent of the lives of its individual members.

But a society is more than the actually-existing arrangement of its constituent groups. Behind this arrangement—or permeating it— there is a whole set of ideas and beliefs which confirm or contradict it. These ideas and beliefs have also a life of their own and they also outlive the individual members of society who are their vehicles. They constitute its collective representations as against its social morphology.

The morphological approach lends itself best to those societies in which collectivities predominate over individuals or where groups have 'a high degree of consistency and constancy'.[4] But even here the accurate representation of the actually-existing groups and their arrangement is by no means easy. For in even the simplest societies the groups are many and various, and they constitute several sets which do not all fit easily into a single scheme.

If the existential order of a society is difficult to describe in simple morphological terms, it is no less difficult to represent its normative order. The components that enter into it are also many and diverse, such as law, morality and religion, to name only a few. It is doubtful if any society has a single comprehensive design or plan of existence that is at any time considered right, proper and desirable by all its individual members. Nevertheless, societies do differ, and differ substantially, in the extent to which equality or its opposite is regarded by religion, law and morality as the acceptable basis of relations between individuals and between groups.

The civilizations of Europe and Asia were in pre-modern times marked by the prominence of ranked social divisions and by the

[3] This approach is the basis of the distinction made by Durkheim between 'segmental' and 'organized' societies in his first book, *The Division of Labour in Society*, The Free Press, 1933 (first published 1893). It is elaborated in Chapter IV, 'Rules for the Classification of Social Types' of his *The Rules of Sociological Method*, The Free Press, 1964 (first published 1895).

[4] The phrase is from E. E. Evans-Pritchard, *The Nuer*, Clarendon Press, 1940,

attention paid to rank in the various spheres of life. The attention to rank was carried over into legal rules and religious beliefs which are in such societies closely intertwined. Moreover, as Tocqueville points out, different standards of right conduct and different conceptions of honour, virtue and even morality are associated with the different ranks or orders into which society is divided.[5] The very terms by which we describe these societies—'aristocratic' society, 'feudal' society, 'hierarchical' society—remind us of the prominence of rank in them.

A very striking feature of these societies, whether in Europe or in Asia, is their idealization of hierarchy. The order of ranks into which society is divided is seen as either a reflection or a segment of a larger, more universal or cosmic hierarchy in which it has its origin and from which it draws its significance. In Hinduism deities were ranked no less than human beings and medieval Christianity, committed as it was to the idea of one God, created or at least embellished an elaborate gradation of celestial beings. Indeed, the word 'hierarchy' derives its primary meaning from the domain of religion where it refers either to ranks of angels or to ranks of ecclesiastical office.

Although in its technical meaning the concept of hierarchy is of Judaeo-Christian origin, the most remarkable historical example of a hierarchical society is Hindu society. The attraction of traditional Hindu society as an example is twofold. Firstly, it has reached closer down to our own times than its counterpart in the West where the erosion of the hierarchical order began well before modern methods of social and historical analysis became established. And secondly, its hierarchical structure, in both its 'morphological' and 'ideological' aspects, was more elaborate, more consistent and more complete than anything known in Western or any other civilization.

The hierarchical order of traditional Indian society was embodied in the institution of caste which has held a commanding position in it for two thousand years. For its sheer durability caste is unparalleled among institutions of its kind. For although the ideological principles

---

p. 262, regarded as one of the most authoritative statements on social structure by a generation of social anthropologists in Britain and elsewhere. Evans-Pritchard developed a somewhat different, more abstract, concept of social structure alongside this morphological one. This has recently been noted by Jack Goody, *Cooking, Cuisine and Class*, Cambridge University Press, 1982, p. 30.

[5] Alexis de Tocqueville, *Democracy in America*, Alfred Knopf, 1956 (first published 1835/1840), vol. 2, especially Third Book, chapter 18.

by which it was justified have been repeatedly attacked and to a large extent supplanted in the last thirty years, the groups which constituted its basic morphological units have held their ground fairly well. It is this remarkable survival of the morphological basis of caste in the face of a major change in ideological alignment that presents perhaps the most serious challenge to planning and nation-building in contemporary India.

Caste has not only been a very durable feature of Indian society, its influence has reached into every segment of its composite structure. In its origin it was a distinctively Hindu institution but it provided an organizational model for all religions that made their home in India. Caste spread its tentacles to the tribal social formations which existed on the margins of Hindu civilization.[6] The Muslims conquered and ruled over large parts of the country for several centuries, but Islamic society in India adapted itself to the morphological pattern of caste.[7] The presence of systems having broadly the same social morphology as caste has been noted in an Islamic cultural environment in Pakistan and in a Buddhist environment in Sri Lanka.[8]

Empirical studies of caste, using modern ethnographic and historical methods of investigation, began in the nineteenth century. The first detailed reports on castes in the various parts of the country were prepared by British civil servants often enough in connection with the census of population. These early investigators were able to witness and record the characteristics of the system while it was still to a large extent intact. From their time till the present we have an unbroken series of studies which enable us to determine with some confidence what is living in the caste system and what is dead.[9]

In talking about caste people talk about two different though interrelated systems which are *varna* and *jati*.[10] *Varna* refers to a

[6] See N. K. Bose, *The Structure of Hindu Society*, Orient Longman, 1975; see also F. G. Bailey, *Tribe, Caste and Nation*, Manchester University Press, 1960.

[7] There is much material, some of it highly controversial, on caste among Indian Muslims. For a recent, fairly balanced selection of viewpoints see Imtiaz Ahmad (ed.), *Caste and Social Stratification among Muslims in India*, Manohar Book Service, second enlarged edition, 1978.

[8] E. R. Leach (ed.), *Aspects of Caste in South India, Ceylon and North-West Pakistan*, Cambridge University Press, 1960.

[9] A useful summary is to be found in David G. Mandelbaum, *Society in India*, University of California Press, 1970, 2 vols.

[10] For a brief distinction between the two see the essay by M. N. Srinivas,

scheme or a conceptual model which divides Hindu society into four categories or orders which are arranged in a hierarchy. The *varna* hierarchy is the same throughout the country and has remained so for roughly two and a half millennia. *Jatis* on the other hand are real social divisions, the groups by which people identify each other in everyday life; they are many in number, and they constitute regional and sometimes only local systems. The popular view that *jatis* originated through division and subdivision of the four original *varnas* is probably wrong; *varna* and *jati* seem to have coexisted since the beginning of Indian history.

Caste in the sense of *jati* divided Indian society into a large number of small, named endogamous groups with clearly-defined and well-recognized boundaries. These divisions (along with the division into men and women) were the most conspicuous morphological features of the small communities, both rural and urban, in which the overwhelming majority of Indians lived. Among Hindus, and to some extent among Muslims and others, the individual had a place in the community less in his own right than as a member of a particular caste. An individual without a caste would be an anachronism, and the divisions of caste were both exclusive and exhaustive. The corporate identity of the caste was kept alive by a variety of rules which were enforced by the subcaste or its local chapter with the backing of the community as a whole.

The social structure of the traditional community, whether village or town, was embodied in its physical structure, physical space and distance reflecting to a large extent social space and social distance.[11] Not only was the community socially divided into different castes, but these castes inhabited different quarters of the village or town in accordance with their social rank. Some castes were socially beyond the pale and they had their dwellings outside the main settlement. The segregation of the 'exterior castes', which is a commonplace of ethnographic descriptions of the Indian village, was in accordance with rules laid down in the *Dharmashastras* and observed for two thousand years.

The maintenance of distance in accordance with social gradation

'*Varna* and Caste' in his *Caste in Modern India and Other Essays*, Asia Publishing House, 1962, pp. 63–9.

[11] For a detailed discussion of the congruence between physical space and social space in an Indian village see André Béteille, *Caste, Class and Power*, University of California Press, 1965.

is an integral part of any hierarchical order. Distances between groups were more strictly and elaborately maintained in India than elsewhere. This became particularly manifest on ceremonial occasions such as temple festivals and marriage feasts. The important thing is that long usage had accustomed people to the unequal places they were required to occupy on all such occasions. The usage was in its turn buttressed by scriptural injunctions of various kinds.

The mechanisms by which distances between groups are maintained in a hierarchical society are the same as those by which these groups maintain their own consistency and constancy. The two most important among these are commensality and connubium. Restrictions on commensality were elaborated to form a central feature of the hierarchical structure of caste. There was firstly the question of who might eat together or sit together for a common meal; over and above this was the question of who might accept food from whom and in what form. Where the structural distance between groups was large, there was no question of reciprocity in the matter of meals, and it was not uncommon for restrictions to be maintained even between groups that were structurally adjacent.

A very common way of maintaining the boundaries between groups is through the restriction of marriage between its members. A system of castes or of estates, or any hierarchical system, cannot be maintained if individuals are left fully free to marry according to their personal choice. The caste system in traditional India carried the restriction of marriage to its extreme, and it has often been maintained that the core of the system as a social system lay in the elaboration of its marriage rules. There were two kinds of rules. There was firstly the general rule of endogamy which required the individual to marry within his own caste or subcaste; this was the preferred rule in both theory and practice. Over and above this was the rule of hypergamy or *anuloma* which allowed men to marry under certain circumstances, in addition to women of their own caste, women from certain prescribed castes regarded as inferior to their own. Hypergamy not only maintains the established ranking of groups, it also confirms the inequality between men and women.

The economy of the village was based on an association between caste and occupation. This association has been observed both when it was fairly strong, as it was a hundred years ago, and when it is breaking down, as it is at present. Individuals were restricted in the occupations they could pursue by the caste to which they belonged although the primary occupation, agriculture, was open to a large number of castes. In general the superior, non-manual occupations were reserved to the highest castes whereas the lowest were burdened with manual and menial occupations.

The different castes not only practised different occupations, they also pursued different styles of life. Differences in styles of life between castes may be observed even today although they are no longer maintained with the same care and attention as in the past. These differences covered a wide range of items from the use of kinship terms to the manner of preparing and serving food. Not all differences were ranked, but some clearly were. Where they were ranked, the confinement to particular styles of life might reflect particular disabilities. For instance, women of the lowest castes were not allowed to wear ornaments of gold and silver or, in the extreme case, even an upper garment.

The hierarchical arrangement of groups was at least among the Hindus supported by a legal order whose broad features showed a remarkable continuity for nearly two thousand years. Muslim rule, which lasted for over five hundred years, did not substantially alter the legal basis of the relations between castes. This began to be affected only after British rule became entrenched in the nineteenth century, and the Constitution of 1950, adopted shortly after independence, instituted a new legal order which was radically different from the old. However, the replacement of the old legal order by a new one did not change everything; and much, or at least some, of the old social morphology has survived even though it is now at odds with the new legal order.

The legal basis of the traditional social order is to be found in the Hindu *Dharmashastras*. The *Dharmashastras* devote attention to the division and subdivision of society into groups, to the origin and basis of these divisions and subdivisions, and to the proper place of each in the scheme of social gradation. It is true that the basic units of the order with which the *Dharmashastras* deal are *varnas* rather than *jatis* which are the basic units of ethnographic description, but they also discuss a variety of specific groupings at least some of which are the forebears of the *jatis* of today.

P. V. Kane, the leading modern authority on the subject, gives a list of over 150 'subcastes' discussed or mentioned in the various

Dharmashastras.[12] As Kane himself points out, the information we get on the various subcastes is highly uneven and often contradictory. The authorities are far from being in complete agreement on the origin, the function or even the rank of each of these various groups. The position is completely different in regard to the four *varnas*: they constitute the immutable order, as it were, of Hindu society as represented in every *Dharmashastra*.

The number of *varnas* and their order of rank are fixed. The *Manusmriti* puts it thus: 'The Brahmana, the Kshatriya, and the Vaisya *varna* are the twice-born ones, but the fourth, the Shudra, has one birth only; there is no fifth.'[13] It is not as if other social groups and divisions are not recognized, but a persistent attempt is made to locate all of these within the fixed framework of the four *varnas*. This framework is universal in its scope, being the basis of social order in all places and at all times.[14] Disorder is nothing but the confusion of *varnas*.

The differentiation of the social world that is represented in the *Dharmashastras* strikes us by its fullness—its 'plenitude'—and its detail. Hardly any course of action is prescribed uniformly for all four *varnas* alike, the proper precedence among them being given careful consideration in virtually everything that is prescribed. The *Manusmriti* gives detailed instructions regarding the paraphernalia to be used in the initiation of members of the three superior *varnas*, indicating separately and in the order of their rank the material to be used for each item by the Brahmins, the Kshatriyas and the Vaishyas, omitting only the Shudras as being unfit for initiation or the dignity of 'second birth'. Even the phrases prescribed for use by the novitiates in seeking alms are varied in accordance with their *varnas*.[15] The spirit behind these instructions is clear even if it proves to be the case that they were not always observed in the letter.

Brahmins and Shudras stand at opposite extremes. Brahmins are showered with extravagant praise: 'Of created beings the most excellent are said to be those which are animated; of the animated, those which subsist by intelligence; of the intelligent, mankind; and

[12] P. V. Kane, *History of Dharmasastra*, Bhandarkar Oriental Research Institute (Poona), second edition, 1974, vol. II, part I, pp. 69–100.

[13] *The Laws of Manu* (trans. G. Buhler), Motilal Banarasidas, 1964, X: 4.

[14] This view of the universal significance of the *varnas* was shared and forcefully expressed in modern times by Mahatma Gandhi. See his *Varnashramadharma*, Navajivan Publishing House (Ahmedabad), 1962.

[15] *The Laws of Manu*, II: 49.

of men, the Brahmins.'[16] The Brahmin receives respect, praise and deference from all others as his due. As to the fourth *varna*, 'One occupation only the lord prescribed to the Shudra, to serve meekly even these (other) three castes.'[17]

The *Dharmashastras* contain much more than a legal code in the strict sense of the term. They represent a moral order as much as a legal order. It has been said that the emphasis in the *Dharmashastras* is on duties and not on rights.[18] Viewed in this light, the privileges and disabilities of caste might appear less oppressive, but privileges and disabilities undoubtedly were of the essence of the system. Indeed, what is striking about the *Dharmashastra* literature as a whole is the emphasis placed on *varna dharma*, the duties of the four *varnas*, as against *sadharana* or *samanya dharma*, the duties common to all alike.

The concept of *dharma*, around which so much of the traditional order of Hindu society turned, is difficult to define. As Mrs Karve has pointed out, it has a naturalistic as well as a normative connotation, signifying both 'necessary attribute' and 'right conduct'.[19] The laws of *dharma* in the broad sense apply to all created beings as well as to men and women. Hierarchical differentiation is to be found not merely among human beings, it animates the whole of creation. The famous Purushasukta hymn, in which the creation of the universe is recounted, assigns to the four *varnas* gods and beasts as well as human beings.

There is a great deal that is fanciful and extravagant in the Hindu theory of *varnas*, and it has been held at fault for being remote from the Indian reality. In a well-known essay, M. N. Srinivas wrote, 'The *varna*-model has produced a wrong and distorted image of caste. It is necessary for the sociologist to free himself from the hold of the *varna*-model if he wishes to understand the caste system.'[20] And again, 'The *varna*-model has been the cause of misinterpretation of the realities of the caste system.'[21] Srinivas was interested in the dynamics of Indian society, and he found the scheme of *varnas* too rigid, too symmetrical and too static to be able to do justice to it.

---

[16] Ibid., I: 96.   [17] Ibid., I: 91.

[18] Kane, *History of Dharmasastra*, vol. II, part I, p. 54.

[19] Irawati Karve, *Hindu Society: An Interpretation*, Deshmukh Prakashan (Poona), second edition, 1968, pp. 91–2.

[20] Srinivas, *Caste in Modern India*, p. 66.

[21] Ibid., p. 67.

There are two important aspects of caste as a social and historical reality that are, according to Srinivas, greatly at variance with the scheme of *varnas*. Firstly, there is and apparently always has been much ambiguity and uncertainty about the actual ranking of *jatis* in contrast to the clear and definite ranking of *varnas*. Secondly, there is the well-known fact of caste mobility, common in recent times but recorded also for the past, in marked opposition to the idea that *varnas* never change their rank. While conceding all this, it would be unwise to deny the claim of reality to something, even if only an idea, that has been acknowledged and endorsed by a whole society, or important sections of it, for two thousand years.

It has been said that *varna* does not signify any real caste, but the idea of caste to which people subscribed.[22] The mere fact that some or, perhaps, many people tried to get their own rank changed or their own caste reclassified does not mean that they repudiated the idea itself of hierarchy or even of the immutable ranking of *varnas*. Some did that as well, but their impact was either not sufficiently strong or not sufficiently lasting, so that the idea of hierarchy continued to govern social life virtually into our own time.[23]

European civilization before modern times had also a hierarchical character, although the hierarchy was less complete, less elaborate and less stable than in the Indian case. It manifested itself in various spheres: in the division of society into estates; in the laws governing their relations; in religious organization, values and beliefs; and in the conception of the world as revealed in art and literature. The hierarchical order attained its most complete form at the end of the Middle Ages—when Europe stood on the threshold of the modern world—animating every important institution, the court, the church, the monastery and the university.

It is doubtful that in Europe the social hierarchy ever acquired the clear outlines that came to characterize it in India. The European

[22] Robert Lingat, *The Classical Law of India*, University of California Press, 1973, puts it thus: 'The word used for caste is varna (literally, "colour"). We shall see that it does *not* signify any real castes, but rather the concept of caste to which our authors subscribed' (pp. 29–30, italics in original).

[23] Our understanding of sectarian movements in India, their true motives and the degrees of their success, is full of gaps. Not all sectarian movements were oriented towards equality, but the egalitarian orientations of some of them, at least in their early phases, can hardly be doubted.

system of estates, which may be considered as the morphological analogue of caste, did not enjoy anything like the life span that caste enjoyed. Moreover, the system varied considerably from one region to another even within Western Europe not only in its formal arrangement but also in its course of growth, maturity and decay. The contrast between France and England—the 'exceptional case of England'—is a commonplace of medieval European history.

The existence and justification of inequality, particularly heredi- tary inequality, is often associated in the popular mind with what is loosely labelled as 'feudalism'. When the *ancien régime* collapsed in France, the rubric of feudalism was employed to point to all its abuses, particularly those against freedom and equality. And of course, popular Marxism, particularly in non-Western countries like India, has done much to represent 'feudalism' and 'capitalism' as two contrastive types of social formation, each with its own type of inequality, maintained by King and Church in the first case and by the market in the second. But European feudalism in the strict sense had only some of the components of hierarchy.[24] By the time a hierarchical social order became fully formed in Europe, feudalism as a distinctive constellation of institutions was clearly in retreat.

The essence of European feudalism lay not so much in the social hierarchy of estates as in the personal tie of dependence between lord and vassal. It must be understood that in its origin, if not in its essence, the feudal relationship of vassalage was a kind of contract which was freely entered into and which both parties, the vassal as well as the lord, were at least in principle free to terminate. Un- doubtedly, there was from the very beginning a difference of rank, and an essential difference of rank, between lord and vassal. But they were not—unlike the *varnas* or the estates which crystallized in European society later—mutually exclusive social groups, so that there was nothing to prevent the same man from being both lord and vassal, though usually to different persons.

The feudal relationship between lord and vassal was in its origin a *personal* relationship between two individuals who were unequal but both free: it was characterized not only by a difference of rank but also by a mutuality of obligation. In course of time it acquired a degree of elaboration. Firstly, what began as a relationship between

[24] As Marc Bloch put it: 'It was an unequal society, rather than a hierarchical one—with chiefs rather than nobles; and with serfs, not slaves' (*Feudal Society*, Routledge and Kegan Paul, 1962, vol. 2, p. 443).

two persons soon grew into a chain of relationships as the vassal acquired his own vassals and these in turn vassals of their own. Secondly, the rights and duties on both sides came to be more formally defined and, with the growing preponderance of the element of property or fief,[25] the relationship lost its free or contractual character and became hereditary.

If we regard the relationship between lord and vassal as the elementary unit of the feudal system, what is of interest from our point of view is the congruence between the objective fact of inequality and the acceptance of it as right, proper and desirable by superior and inferior alike. Objectively, the vassal was his lord's inferior in wealth, power and prestige, not in every case, but certainly in the typical case. The recognition of this by both parties constituted the basis of the feudal relationship. The inequality between lord and vassal was expressed by a whole array of symbols, and this symbolism coloured every kind of relationship in feudal society.

Feudalism combined the general acceptance of a hierarchical basis for personal relations with a degree of contention and strife between master and man over the actual claims of each in relation to the other. The vassal might bend his knee before his lord as a matter of sacred duty, or hold his stirrup as the lord mounted his horse; but that was no guarantee that the lord's authority would never be challenged or even repudiated by his vassal. The annals of medieval Europe are full of accounts of dukes challenging their king's authority, of barons challenging their duke's authority and of knights challenging their baron's authority; all of this within a moral framework in which the hierarchy of king, duke, baron and knight was implicitly accepted by all.[26]

We have to remember that feudalism emerged in Europe in unsettled times, under unsettled conditions, and feudal institutions carried the marks of these conditions into a later age when conditions had become relatively settled and the social order relatively stable. Individual mobility must have occurred widely in the early stages of feudalism when fortunes were commonly made or unmade in the field of battle, and barriers between classes and estates had not be-

[25] I follow Ganshof in assigning priority to the 'personal' over the 'property' element in defining the feudal relationship. F. L. Ganshof, *Feudalism*, Harper and Row, 1964.

[26] The pattern is very familiar to students of English literature through the historical novels of Walter Scott and the historical plays of Shakespeare.

come clear. In course of time the order of ranks became stable and with this stability went the transmission of rank by hereditary succession. The scope for individual mobility became restricted, although such mobility was never completely ruled out in either practice or theory.

While the distinction between lord and vassal formed the social basis of feudalism, this distinction did not lead automatically or at once to the formation of a social estate of noblemen. Marc Bloch has told us what constitutes a nobility in the proper sense: 'First, it must have a legal status of its own, which confirms and makes effectual the superiority to which it lays claim. In the second place, this status must be hereditary—with the qualification, however, that a limited number of families may be admitted to it, in accordance with formally established rules.'[27] The nobility in this sense emerged late in Western Europe and did not become established as a social estate until 'the fief and vassalage were already in decline'.[28] In other words, a hierarchy of estates replaced in course of time a chain of personal positions.

As conditions became settled, the nobility closed its ranks, defined and enlarged its privileges and developed its own style of life. According to Bloch, 'the period from about 1250 to about 1400 was, on the continent, the period which witnessed the most rigid stratification of social classes.'[29] There were considerable variations in the actual pattern of stratification in both space and time. Even between France and England, neighbours who shared many things in common, there were important differences. The nobility never acquired in England the array of privileges it enjoyed in France, and English historians frequently point to the antiquity of their own traditions of equality.[30] But for all its distinctiveness, England also developed a social hierarchy, many elements of which lasted longer there than in other West European countries.[31]

Wherever society took on the character of a stable hierarchy, the

[27] Bloch, *Feudal Society*, vol. 2, p. 283.
[28] Ibid., p. 283.   [29] Ibid., p. 325.
[30] Maitland is a well-known example. See F. Pollock and F. W. Maitland, *The History of English Law before the Time of Edward I*, Cambridge University Press, second edition, 1968; see also Alan Macfarlane, *The Origins of English Individualism*, Basil Blackwell, 1978.
[31] As recently as a hundred years ago, Matthew Arnold was castigating the English on their 'religion of inequality'. See his essay on 'Equality' in Matthew Arnold, *Mixed Essays*, John Murray, popular edition, 1903, pp. 48–97.

privileges of the nobility were also the privileges of birth. Noble birth came to be invested with a special quality, not to say sanctity, in poetry, in social convention and even in law. Marriage among the nobility became to some extent—although never to the same extent as in the case of caste—an institution for preserving and refining the purity of noble blood; and there grew a kind of opposition between the institution of marriage and the ideal of romantic love, centering around the conventions of chivalry.

The nobility created for itself a variety of privileges, immunities and exemptions. Some occupations were reserved for noblemen and others were forbidden to them if not by law at least by custom; in the extreme case, not unlike in caste society, the nobleman lost his rank by derogation if he pursued an occupation considered to be beneath his station. The nobleman not only lived well in a material sense, he lived with dignity and grace, according to the accepted conceptions of his time. It is true that he lived largely at the expense of others, but the splendour and magnificence of his life tinged also the lives of these others.

No account of the social hierarchy in medieval Europe will be adequate without some attention being paid, however briefly, to the social situation of the serf: the privileges of nobles are in this kind of social order balanced by the disabilities of serfs. For one influential group of writers it is neither vassalage nor the fief, but serfdom that constitutes the defining feature of feudalism. Serfdom is in this perspective viewed as 'an obligation laid on the producer by force and independently of his own volition to fulfil certain economic demands of an overlord, whether the demands take the form of services to be performed or of dues to be paid in money or in kind'.[32] Serfs were in medieval Europe typically peasants, and serfdom was in the strict sense a legal condition, but the disabilities imposed by that condition on the peasants did not all disappear as soon as they were made legally free.

The striking thing about the medieval peasantry is that a large section of it was servile. Maitland, writing about England in the thirteenth century, tells us that 'the greater half of the rural population is unfree'.[33] The unfree peasant had not only his conditions of labour but also his personal life regulated by his master. In relation to his master he was not a legal person: he could neither sue nor be

[32] Maurice Dobb, *Studies in the Development of Capitalism*, Routledge and Kegan Paul, 1963, p. 35.
[33] Pollock and Maitland, *The History of English Law*, vol. 1, p. 432.

sued by him, although he did have rights in relation to others. In general he could not hold public office. A serf could not be knighted, and a serf knighted by mistake could be degraded if his servile status was proved. Also, it was forbidden by both canon law and civil law to ordain a serf.[34]

The status of serf, like that of nobleman, was acquired largely by birth. The custom was for serfs to marry serfs although exceptions frequently occurred. When a serf married a free person there was some uncertainty as to the status of the offspring, although Maitland refers to a rule approved by the church that 'whenever free and servile blood are mixed, the servile prevails'.[35] The concern over the rank to be assigned to the offspring of mixed unions is characteristic of hierarchical societies. This concern is seen in its extreme, one may say obsessive, form in the Hindu *Dharmashastras* where the consequences of mixed unions are argued through with unsurpassed dialectical zeal.

The social world of medieval Europe was not made up of only noblemen and serfs. It was a world of many gradations. There were class distinctions within the peasantry and there were free and unfree peasants. There was the clerical estate, itself elaborately graded and meeting at many points the gradations of the lay estate. Then there were the merchants and craftsmen whose increasing wealth and power were not reflected in the rank they were assigned in society and which in the Middle Ages they by and large accepted.

This hierarchical society with its many gradations attained its most complete form at the end of the Middle Ages and continued well into early modern times. Lucien Febvre has given us a graphic description of social gradations in the typical community in sixteenth-century France:

> The Church was the center to which men rallied in times of danger and in times of joy. Every Sunday and every feast day saw the whole community assembled together, in hierarchical order. The men of the cloth were in the choir. In the seigneurial pew way up front, were the gentry, milord with his dogs, his wife, and his children. The magistrates stiffened with peasant dignity sat just behind them, then the laborers, and finally the humble folk, the valets, servants, children, and animals which were just as much at ease in the church as anywhere else.[36]

---

[34] Ibid., p. 429.   [35] Ibid., p. 422.
[36] Lucien Febvre, *Life in Renaissance France*, Harvard University Press, 1977, p. 74. Lawrence Stone's account of Early Modern England describes 'the socially

It was not only in the church that the social hierarchy was physically displayed; it was also displayed in the manor house, particularly at meal-times and specially on feast days.

Social life in pre-modern times had a personal and intimate character, and social distinctions were made visible to all by outward marks. The preoccupation with outward and visible symbols of dignity received expression in elaborately stylized forms of dress: 'Through all the ranks of society a severe hierarchy of material and colour kept classes apart, and gave to each estate or rank an outward distinction, which preserved and exalted the feeling of dignity.'[37] In course of time the symbolism of ranks came to have a life of its own. In France and Burgundy the lying-in chambers of ladies had colours according to their ranks: green was the colour of queens and princesses, forbidden even to countesses. Distinctions of rank were observed even when a man was sent to the scaffold: 'the scaffold mounted by the Constable of Saint-Pol is richly shrouded with black velvet strewn with fleurs-de-lis; the cloth with which his eyes are bandaged, the cushion on which he kneels are of crimson velvet.'[38]

Social distinctions were made visible by much more than the colour and material of dress and decoration. The whole pomp and ceremony of courtly life, developed into an art in the courts of France and Burgundy in the later Middle Ages, was adjusted to fine if not subtle distinctions of rank. Courtly life gave affirmation to rank by regulating precedence in minute detail on every occasion: in receiving guests, in seating them at table, in addressing them and attending to them. The ideals of courtly life were not confined to the royal court or the ducal court; and they long outlived the Middle Ages.

Giving form and significance to all these details of everyday life and ceremonial observance was what Huizinga has described as 'the hierarchic conception of society'. This conception is, in Huizinga's presentation of it, basically a religious and an aesthetic conception

---

graded arrangements for seating in churches, with the squirearchy hidden behind their high box pews in the chancel, the middle ranks placed at the upper end of the nave, each within his family pew, and the poor clustered on benches at the back'. Lawrence Stone, *The Family, Sex and Marriage in England 1500–1800*, Weidenfeld and Nicholson, 1977, p. 222.

[37] J. Huizinga, *The Waning of the Middle Ages*, Edward Arnold, 1924, p. 43.
[38] Ibid., p. 34. The Count of Saint-Pol, Constable of France, who became embroiled in the conflict between Louis XI of France and Charles the Bold of Burgundy, was executed on 19 December 1475.

which came to suffuse life in the Middle Ages, reaching into every area of it by the end of the fifteenth century. The idea of 'estate' may be considered as the unit idea in the hierarchic conception of society. The term 'estate' does not have a single referent, it has many referents: several kinds of estates are described in accounts of the same society.[39] What gave unity to the idea was the belief that estates and their order of rank, wherever they occurred, were divine institutions rather than human artifices.

In a conception which regards the orders of society as divine rather than human institutions, the value of each order 'will not depend on its utility, but on its sanctity'.[40] Here we find a striking similarity between the European theory of estates and the Hindu theory of *varnas* where also utility is subordinated to sanctity or, at any rate, to purity. Like the *varnas*, the estates are viewed as being not only divinely instituted but also eternal: 'The estates of society cannot but be venerable and lasting, because they all have been ordained by God. The conception of society in the Middle Ages is statical, not dynamical.'[41]

The idea of equality was not unknown to the Middle Ages, but, Huizinga tells us, it was not taken very seriously as a basis for the regulation of social life. In both church sermon and lay poetry, equality was most frequently remembered in the context of death: it was death alone which cancelled the distinctions of rank, death being no doubt a common preoccupation in the medieval world. The Catholic church was hardly a strong advocate of equality here and now. The sixteenth-century French moralist and theologian, Jean Benedicti, wrote, 'Those who violate the laws and just commands of their superiors, believing and saying that men are by nature equal and of the same condition, without some having authority over

[39] 'The idea of an "estate" is not at all limited to that of a class; it extends to every social function, to every profession, to every group. Side by side with the French system of the three estates of the realm, which in England, according to Professor Pollard, was only secondarily and theoretically adopted after the French model, we find traces of a system of twelve social estates. The functions or groupings, which the Middle Ages designated by the words "estate" and "order", are of very diverse natures. There are, first of all, the estates of the realm, but there are also the trades, the state of matrimony and that of virginity, the state of sin. At court there are the "four estates of body and mouth": bread-masters, cup-bearers, carvers and cooks. In the Church there are sacerdotal orders and monastic orders. Finally, there are the different orders of chivalry' (ibid., p. 47).
[40] Ibid., p. 48.   [41] Ibid., p. 48.

6

others, are heretics.'[42] Church dignitaries took little trouble over the maxim of Gregory the Great: *Omnes namque homines natura aequales sumus.*[43]

The hierarchical conception of society did not disappear from Europe with the passing of the Middle Ages. A student of Elizabethan and early Stuart England has written:

> Hierarchy and organic unity were the two predominant postulates upon which contemporaries constructed their theories about the nature of society and the functions of government. As the universe was ordered in a great chain of being, so the nation was regulated by obedience to a hierarchy of superiors leading up to the King, so society was composed of various estates of men all settled and contented in their degree, and so the family was ordered by obedience of wife and children to the *pater familias.*[44]

But this conception had increasingly to contend with other conceptions of man and society shaped by the powerful intellectual currents set in motion by the Reformation in the sixteenth century and by the Enlightenment in the seventeenth and eighteenth centuries.

The idea of a universal hierarchy in which each created being has its appointed place was expressed by Alexander Pope in his widely-read *Essay on Man* (1733–34):

> Order is Heav'n's first law; and this confest,
> Some are, and must be, greater than the rest,
> More rich, more wise; but who infers from hence
> That such are happier, shocks all common sense.
> Heav'n to Mankind impartial we confess,
> If all are equal in their Happiness:
> But mutual wants this Happiness increase;
> All Nature's diff'rence keeps all Nature's peace.[45]

---

[42] Quoted in Jean-Louis Flandrin, *Families in Former Times*, Cambridge University Press, 1979, p. 120.

[43] 'For all of us, human beings, are equal by nature'. Gregory the Great (540–604), saint and pope, is said to have been the architect of the medieval papacy.

[44] Lawrence Stone, *The Crisis of the Aristocracy 1558–1641*, Clarendon Press, 1965, p. 21. Stone goes on to add, 'In fact as late as 1870 England was basically aristocratic in tone, taking its moral standards, its hierarchy of social values, and its political system from the landed classes' (ibid.).

[45] Alexander Pope, *Essay on Man*, IV: 49–56. Compare Shakespeare,
> The heavens themselves, the planets, and this centre
> Observe degree, priority, and place,
> Insisture, course, proportion, season, form,
> Office, and custom, in all line of order;

Troilus and Cressida, I. iii. 85–8.

We see already a difference of mood: all men are in some fundamental sense equal not because they must all submit to death but
because they all have, irrespective of their station in society, the
capacity for happiness. After 1789 it became difficult if not impossible
to denounce the claim 'that men are by nature equal and of the same
condition' as heretical.

Pope's *Essay on Man* gave expression to a conception that was very
widely held in the eighteenth century. This is the conception of the
Great Chain of Being which, according to Arthur O. Lovejoy, was
until recent times 'probably the most widely familiar conception of
the general *scheme* of things, of the constitutive pattern of the universe'.[46] The conception of the Great Chain of Being is essentially a
religious conception which medieval Christianity took over from
neo-Platonism and shaped to its own requirement. It was given its
most general and abstract expression by the philosophers of the
seventeenth and eighteenth centuries, notably Spinoza and Leibnitz.

The conception of the Great Chain of Being is in its essence a
hierarchical conception, although its concern is not so much with
the divisions of men in society as with the universal hierarchy within
which men and their society have a very small, though by no means
insignificant, place. Indeed, what gives significance to man, by no
means the noblest of created beings, is the *necessary* place he takes in
the universal scheme of things; just as what gives significance to the
meanest peasant is the necessary part *he* plays in the community as
a whole. The three essential components of the conception are,
according to Lovejoy, 'plenitude', 'continuity' and 'linear gradation':
the universe has to be full, vacancies cannot occur, all places exist by
necessity; but all places are not equal in worth or dignity, there
being a continuous and infinite gradation of dignity and worth
according to proximity to the godhead.

Hobbes and Locke had argued the case for equality in the seventeenth century, but it was left to the philosophers and publicists of
the eighteenth century—Rousseau, Voltaire and others in France—
to take the offensive in the cause of equality, attacking and denounc-
ing every traditional argument in support of hierarchy and privilege.
The French Revolution became the turning point, to the extent that
any historical event may be regarded as a turning point in matters so
complex and full of contradiction. It destroyed the hierarchical conception of society as a living thing, although that conception was to

[46] Arthur O. Lovejoy, *The Great Chain of Being*, Harvard University Press,
1964, p. vii.

survive for some more time as a form of nostalgia. After the French Revolution the case for hierarchy ceased to appear self-evident; more and more people began to argue about social arrangements from the premise of equality between persons.

The social world of medieval Europe or traditional India was different from the modern world, whether in Europe or in India. The idea of a fixed order of rank among persons, corresponding to a larger, a universal order of rank, has lost its hold over the minds of Europeans and is losing its hold over the minds of Indians. Indians and Europeans can perhaps still reconstruct mentally the hierarchical orders of the past for there are still many marks of these, faint or clear, in present-day institutions. Americans and Australians may find it difficult to do even that for theirs are new societies which Europeans constructed in other lands when their own traditional hierarchies were already in retreat.

The first and in some ways still the most outstanding contrast between the hierarchical social order of the past and the emerging social order with its commitment to equality was the one made by Alexis de Tocqueville. Tocqueville's contrast between aristocracy and democracy is not confined to two modes of political organization; it extends to patterns of social distinction, forms of religious experience and consciousness, and types of aesthetic sensibility. Although born a few years after the French Revolution, he came from an aristocratic family, one which had suffered by it, and he spoke of the life and ideals of the aristocracy with the insight of personal knowledge. On the other hand, democracy still lay largely in the future, although the promise of that future infused his writing with an astonishingly vivid quality.

The flaw in Tocqueville's writing seems to lie in this, that the terms of the contrast between aristocracy and democracy are for him symmetrical whereas, in the light of our closer experience of democracy, they are not. It is this lack of symmetry between 'aristocratic' and 'democratic' societies, or between 'hierarchical' and 'egalitarian' societies, that I have sought to represent by the contrast between harmonic and disharmonic social systems.

In talking about aristocracy Tocqueville drew attention to the elaborate gradations of rank as well as the general acceptance of these gradations by people in all stations of life as a part of the natural scheme of things. He dwelt in particular on the organic character of aristocratic societies: 'Among aristocratic nations all the members of the community are connected with and dependent upon each other; the graduated scale of different ranks acts as a tie which keeps everyone in his proper place and the whole body in subordination.'[47] And he uses the metaphor of the Chain of Being with great felicity: 'Aristocracy had made a chain of all the members of the community, from the peasant to the king.'[48] There was harmony between the external conditions of life and the socially accepted ideals of life.

Democratic society, as Tocqueville saw it, was not only oriented towards a radically different ideal of social life, it was also in the process of creating a radically new framework of material existence. Tocqueville saw the new society as one in which the social ideal of equality would be substantially if not fully matched by equality of material condition.[49] Democratic society was not only levelling out differences of rank, it was equalizing the distribution of fortunes as well.

Tocqueville maintained that there was more equality of condition in democratic than in aristocratic societies and that this equality would increase in the course of time. But by 'equality of condition' he meant various things: not only equality before the law and the absence of ranks but also economic equality and the absence of extremes of wealth and poverty. The poor are 'comparatively few in number', and the wealthy are 'few and powerless'. 'Between these two extremes of democratic communities stands an innumerable multitude of men almost alike, who, without being exactly either rich or poor, possess sufficient property to desire the maintenance of order, yet not enough to excite envy.'[50] Equality of condition means also that individuals are able to move across class barriers with such ease that class distinctions virtually lose their social significance.

Now, we know today that the kinds of forces that level out distinctions of rank and bring about legal equality, and those that

[47] Tocqueville, *Democracy in America*, vol. 2, p. 89.

[48] Ibid., vol. 2, p. 99.

[49] He was shrewd enough to realize that in such a society even small inequalities of condition might lead to large discontent: 'When inequality of conditions is the common law of society, the most marked inequalities do not strike the eye; when everything is nearly on the same level, the slightest are marked enough to hurt it' (ibid., vol. 2, p. 138).

[50] Ibid., vol. 2, p. 252.

reduce wealth and poverty, and bring about economic equality do not move at all according to the same rhythm. Certainly, as far as the United States is concerned, inequality of condition in the sense of economic inequality or inequality in the distribution of wealth and income, has not declined between Tocqueville's time and our own. If anything, it increased in the hundred years since he visited the country; and if there has been any appreciable decrease in it in the last fifty years, the trends of change do not by any means point clearly in one direction.

Class distinctions have not disappeared from America, and American society has not become a 'classless society', not even a 'middle-class society'. Despite the idealization of equality, the class structure continues to be an important part of Western social reality, some would say its most important part. It is true that the outlines of the class structure are complex and confusing, but that such a structure exists and that it contains within itself mechanisms for its own reproduction can hardly be contested. Only this structure is no longer a structure of privileges and disabilities, but one of unequal life chances.

Inequalities in the distribution of life chances result from various causes and are reproduced in various ways. They also differ greatly in degree from one society to another. These inequalities are particularly marked in contemporary India where new distinctions of class coexist with the old distinctions of caste. The marks of both caste and class are visibly present in rural as well as urban communities. Caste distinctions are still clearly seen in the settlement pattern of most villages where, despite changes in ideology, the lowest and the highest castes continue to be residentially segregated to a large extent. Caste is less conspicuous in the cities where distinctions of wealth and poverty are the most visible features of the settlement pattern.

The visible presence of caste and class in the social morphology rests uneasily with the ideal expressed in the Indian Constitution of a 'casteless and classless society'. The equality provisions in the Constitution are many, varied and far-reaching. The preoccupation with equality in it is no less remarkable than the preoccupation with ranking and gradation in the *Dharmashastras*. Nor is it confined only to the Constitution, although it would be rash to conclude that this new-found preoccupation has cancelled out every mode of consciousness inherited from the past. What is nevertheless striking is that one encounters in India today hardly any sustained intellectual defence of inequality in the form of either caste or class.

It is a commonplace of text-books of sociology that class is a *de facto* system unlike estate (or caste) which is a *de jure* system. In the second half of the twentieth century people acquiesce in or, at best, defend distinctions of class, they do not actively espouse them; and, to revert to Huizinga's phrase, class distinctions are defended on grounds of utility, never on grounds of sanctity. There is something half-hearted, not to say shamefaced, about the defence of class in contrast to the defence of equality, or liberty, or even efficiency. It would be hardly an exaggeration to say that there is a perpetual crisis of legitimation hanging over the class structure of every modern society. It is to this crisis of legitimation so palpable in present-day India, rather than to any past state of bliss, that I wished to draw attention by making the contrast between harmonic and disharmonic social systems.

The Backward Classes and the New Social Order*

The B. R. Ambedkar Memorial Lectures, 1980

I

I would like to devote these lectures to the problem of the Backward Classes in the new social order. In electing to do so I have in mind the concern felt for the problem by the person whose memory we are here to honour as well as the intrinsic importance of the subject itself. It is a subject that has a practical and a theoretical side, and if I choose to dwell especially on the latter, it is in the belief that action can be fruitful only if it is informed by proper understanding. A proper understanding of the problem of the Backward Classes requires us to view it in several perspectives, notably those of the social sciences and of legal studies; for we are at every step confronted by the divergence between what exists as social reality and what ought to exist according to the laws we have created for ourselves.

Put in a somewhat different way, what I propose to do may be described as a sociological critique of the equality provisions in the Constitution of India. These provisions are both wide-ranging and varied. We cannot understand either their scope or their complexity in terms of purely formal principles. We can appreciate their nature and significance only by relating them to the historical background from which they have emerged and the social context to which they were designed to apply.

No society can move forward unless it sets for itself an ideal of achievement that is superior to the present reality. To this extent the design for living enshrined in a Constitution must rise above the social arrangements that exist on the ground. At the same time, it

* I am much indebted to Dr B. Sivaramayya for his help and encouragement in the preparation of these essays.

cannot afford to lose touch with the social facts as they are. For these facts are not only there, but they exercise constraints that cannot be wished out of existence. A Constitution may indicate the direction in which we are to move, but the social structure will decide how far we are able to move and at what pace.

A society has thus to be judged both for what it is and for what it wishes to be. A written Constitution, and especially one that is written at a decisive turn in its history, has a certain significance as an expression of what a society seeks to achieve for itself. A very striking feature of our Constitution is its stress on equality. It is present in the Preamble; it is present in the part embodying the Fundamental Rights; and it is present in the part laying down the Directive Principles of State Policy. Legislative enactments and judicial pronouncements have during the last three decades reiterated this commitment over and over again.

Jurists have pointed out how we have gone further than most modern Constitutions, including the American, in inscribing the commitment to equality into ours. Thus, in speaking of the guarantee of equality, P. K. Tripathi says, 'But it must be appreciated that the scope of the guarantee in the Constitution of India extends far beyond either, or both, the English and the United States guarantees taken together.'[1] One has only to go through the record of debates in the Constituent Assembly, or to examine the notes and memoranda prepared by members of the Assembly and by the Constitutional Adviser to see how strong the preoccupation with equality was among the makers of the Indian Constitution. This preoccupation was itself a part of a historical process that grew with the movement for freedom from colonial bondage.

Despite all this, our practice continues to be permeated by inequality in every sphere. The marks of inequality are visible in every form of collective life. Our rural and urban communities are divided and subdivided into groups and categories that are ranked in elaborate gradations. The distinctions among castes and among classes, though no longer upheld by the law, are taken into account everywhere. There are numerous barriers between the strata, and they are difficult to cross. The reality of rigid social stratification makes itself felt in the daily lives of the poor and the oppressed in general and the Untouchables in particular.

[1] P. K. Tripathi, *Some Insights into Fundamental Rights*, University of Bombay, 1972, p. 47.

The problem of the Backward Classes is, in its most general form, the problem of achieving equality in a world permeated by inequality. The significance of the category 'Backward Classes' lies not only in its size and extent, but also in the uniquely Indian way of defining its boundaries. This uniqueness is a reflection of specific social and historical conditions. In India, unlike in other societies, 'backwardness' is viewed as an attribute not of individuals but of communities which are, by their nature, self-perpetuating. In ordinary sociological discourse a class is a set of individuals—or, at best, families—sharing certain life chances in common that they may or may not owe to their ancestors, and that they may or may not transmit to their descendants. By the terms of that discourse, the Backward Classes are not classes at all, but groups of communities.

Judicial pronouncements on the subject reflect the ambiguity inherent in the situation. There are judgements, as in the famous *Balaji's* case, which imply that there is, or ought to be, a clear distinction between 'caste' and 'class'.[2] There are other judgements which maintain, as in *Rajendran's* case, that 'a caste is also a class of citizens',[3] or, more strongly, as in *Periakaruppan's* case, that 'A caste has always been recognized as a class'.[4] The discrepancy between the two views is in part, but only in part, due to the use in the first case of a 'sociological' conception of class, and in the second, of what may be called a 'logical' or purely formal conception of it. But the ambiguity is not merely terminological; its roots lie deeper, in our traditional social structure, and in our contemporary attitudes to it.

The Backward Classes are a large and mixed category of persons with boundaries that are both unclear and elastic. Together, they comprise roughly one-third of the total population of the country. They are made up of three principal components, the Scheduled Tribes, the Scheduled Castes and the other Backward Classes. The Scheduled Tribes and the Scheduled Castes are well-defined categories, comprising respectively a little less than seven and a little more than fourteen per cent of the population. The Other Backward Classes are a residual category; their position is highly ambiguous; and it is impossible to give an exact statement of their number.

The Backward Classes provide a window into modern Indian

[2] M. R. Balaji *vs* State of Mysore (*A.I.R. 1963 S.C.* 649).
[3] P. Rajendran *vs* State of Madras (*A.I.R. 1968 S.C.* 1012).
[4] A. Periakaruppan *vs* State of Tamil Nadu (*A.I.R. 1973 S.C.* 2310).

society as a whole. It has been said about the traditional order of Hindu society that it was so extensively marked by the pre-eminence of the Brahmin that an understanding of his social situation provided a key to the understanding of its structure as a whole.[5] In many ways the Backward Classes occupy such a privileged position in contemporary Indian society from the point of view of method. For if our interest is in the interplay between equality and hierarchy, there is no significant problem that can escape us if we fix our attention on these sections of Indian society.

If we are to understand how far the law can be used as an instrument of social change, we have to begin by recognizing the disharmony between the legal order with its commitment to complete equality and the social order with its all-pervasive stratification. This disharmony has to be examined in the widest historical and comparative perspective. All modern societies have, in the broadest sense, to contend with the problem of reconciling the ideal of equality with the facts of inequality. It is to this aspect of the modern world that a distinguished European sociologist drew attention when he wrote, 'Modern industrial societies are both egalitarian in aspiration and hierarchical in organization.'[6]

We can better appreciate the paradox of equality in contemporary Indian society by comparing it with other contemporary societies and by contrasting it with societies of the past. We take the ideal of equality so much for granted today that we tend to overlook the point that traditional societies were hierarchical not only in fact but also by design. As Isaiah Berlin had pointed out in a well-known essay on Equality, 'Classical thought seems to be deeply and "naturally" inegalitarian';[7] and both Aristotle and Plato believed in a natural hierarchy of persons, and insisted on appropriate differences of treatment for each of its various levels. Medieval Europe also regarded its hierarchical order to be a part of the natural scheme of things; and, standing on the threshold of the modern world,

[5] See, for instance, L. Dumont, *Homo Hierarchicus: The Caste System and Its Implications*, Paladin 1972. Max Weber also was inclined to argue that the key to the understanding of Hindu society lay in the social situation of the Brahmin; see his *The Religion of India*, The Free Press, 1958.

[6] R. Aron, *Progress and Disillusion*, Pall Mall Press, 1968, p. xv.

[7] I. Berlin, 'Equality' in his *Concepts and Categories: Philosophical Essays*, Hogarth Press, 1978, p. 99.

Tocqueville presented a luminous contrast between the 'aristocratic' societies of the past and the 'democratic' societies of the future.[8]

The spirit of hierarchy had its most luxuriant growth in our own traditional society, with its concrete embodiment in the institutions of *varna* and *jati*. Some have been so greatly struck by the stress on hierarchy in the traditional Hindu system of values that they have questioned whether there was in it any appreciation at all of equality as a value. This is to carry a reasonable argument to an unreasonable conclusion, for religious discourse in India never wholly abandoned a concern for man as man, the human spirit behind the external markers of social entitlement and worldly achievement. It is this side of Indian religiosity that attracted Mahatma Gandhi to the message of the Gita and Dr Ambedkar to the teaching of the Buddha.

But it has to be admitted that the idea of equality was for the most part narrowly confined to what may be described as the realm of the spirit. It is difficult from our point of view to see how much solace a man crushed by the burden of an oppressive hierarchy could receive from the thought that his ultimate claim to salvation was as good as that of any other man. At any rate, we have to make a distinction between the spiritual order and the legal order, even though, in a traditional society, both receive their ultimate sanction from religion. In considering the legal order of a society we are less concerned with its ultimate values than with the values that justify and uphold its existing institutions.

The legal order of traditional Hindu society is embodied in the *Dharmashastras*. I am neither a legal scholar nor a classical scholar, but one does not have to be either to see how radically different their spirit is from the spirit of our Constitution. It can hardly be an accident that the man primarily responsible for its drafting chose as an act of public protest to burn the *Manusmriti* which for two thousand years occupied a pre-eminent position among the *Dharmashastras*.

Shudras and women are marked out in the *Dharmashastras* for indignities of every conceivable kind. They are dealt with more strictly than others; their disabilities are grave and onerous; and they are debarred from most of the ordinary graces of life. The subordination of women is underscored in a well-known verse in the

---

[8] A. de Tocqueville, *Democracy in America*, Alfred Knopf, 1956; see also my Kingsley Martin Memorial Lecture, 'Homo Hierarchicus, Homo Equalis', republished in this volume, pp. 33–53.

Manusmriti: 'In childhood a female must be subject to her father, in youth to her husband, when her lord is dead to her sons; a woman must never be independent.'[9] The Shudra's lot is not much better: 'A Shudra, though emancipated by his master, is not released from servitude; since this is innate in him, who can set him free from it?'[10] Even as sympathetic a reader of the *Dharmashastras* as P. V. Kane was obliged to concede that 'the life of a Shudra was not worth much'.[11]

It would be a mistake to try to account for all this by means of a narrow theory of interests. Some of the injunctions in the *Dharmashastras* are plainly designed to safeguard the interests of the privileged at the expense of the underprivileged. Others seem to express pure and unalloyed malice, as, for instance, the one against the acquisition of wealth by the Shudras on the ground that 'a Shudra who has acquired wealth gives pain to Brahmins'.[12] Above all, one is struck by the luxuriant growth of the discriminatory process which had, in the manner of tropical vegetation, spread in every direction, leaving no ground uncovered.

The Shudras themselves did not remain an undifferentiated category. They became differentiated into superior and inferior, and the discrimination which the Brahmins practised against them was in turn practised by the superior Shudras against the inferior. Shudras came to be dichotomized in several ways, of which Kane mentions three: the dichotomy of *sat-* and *asat-*Shudras (well- and ill-conducted Shudras); of *bhojyanna* and *abhojyanna* Shudras (those from whom food may or may not be accepted); and of *aniravasita* and *niravasita* Shudras ('clean' and 'unclean' Shudras).[13] In course of time the last came to be regarded as a separate category, outside the pale of the four *varnas*.

It was for the *niravasita* Shudras—the Chandalas and the Shvapachas—that the worst indignities were reserved. They are the classical forebears of the Scheduled Castes of today. Manu requires that 'the

---

[9] *The Laws of Manu* (trans. G. Buhler), Motilal Banarsidas, 1964, V: 148. Or, again, 'Her father protects her in childhood, her husband protects her in youth, and her sons protect her in old age; a woman is never fit for independence' (ibid. IX: 3).

[10] Ibid., VIII: 414.

[11] P. V. Kane, *History of Dharmasastras*, Bhandarkar Oriental Research Institute (Poona), vol. 2, part I, 1974, p. 163.

[12] *The Laws of Manu*, X: 129.

[13] Kane, *History of Dharmasastras*, vol. 2, part I, pp. 121–2.

dwellings of Chandalas and Shvapachas shall be outside the village ... their dress the garments of the dead ... their food ... given to them ... in a broken dish'.[14] Again, what strikes one in all this is not simply that distinctions should be made between superior and inferior, or that they should be made primarily according to birth, but that they should seek to leave no sphere of life free from their impress.

It is a familiar argument among sociologists that no society could possibly function if all the injunctions laid down in the *Dharmashastras* were actually to be practised. More than a hundred years ago, Sir Henry Maine had endorsed the view that the *Manusmriti* 'does not, as a whole, represent a set of rules ever actually administered in Hindostan', adding that 'It is, in great part, an ideal picture of that which, in the view of the Brahmins, *ought* to be the law.'[15] Custom and common sense obviously played a part in protecting the system from its own absurd conclusions. The fact remains, however, that attitudes towards existing social divisions were radically different then from what they are now; at the same time, many of these social divisions persist, despite the change in spirit encoded in our new legal order. This is the most manifest contradiction in everyday life in contemporary India.

It is easy enough to see the contradiction between the ideal of equality and the practice of inequality. What is far less obvious is that the idea of equality is itself made up of various components which cannot be assumed to be always mutually consistent. It might indeed be argued that one reason why there is disharmony between ideal and reality in the modern world is that the concept of equality is itself heterogeneous. I believe that the makers of our Constitution had some awareness of this and of the need to strive for a harmonious construction of the different components of the concept, although there cannot be, in the very nature of the case, any simple formula for achieving such a construction.

The concept of equality is so wide in scope and has had such diverse historical expressions that it would be surprising if it retained a single, univocal meaning. Like all such basic and fundamental concepts, it is both equivocal and inexhaustible. The makers of our Constitution took great pains to incorporate into it whatever they

[14] *The Laws of Manu*, X: 51–2.
[15] H. S. Maine, *Ancient Law*, Oxford University Press, 1950, p. 14.

found to be of value in the democratic constitutions of the modern world. They were, in my view, right in doing this, even though breadth of scope had to be achieved at some cost to unity of conception.

Very broadly considered, one can distinguish between equality in the simple sense and equality considered as a ratio. This is an old distinction in Western ethical and political philosophy, and Aristotle makes it both in his *Ethics* and in his *Politics*. In his terminology, the distinction is between 'numerical' equality and 'proportional' equality; as he puts it, 'by the first I mean sameness or equality in number or size; by the second equality of ratios'.[16] Aristotle deals primarily with 'proportional' equality, and his whole theory of distributive justice is based on it.

Equality in the simple sense takes no account of the differences among people. It distributes values in such a way that no recipient gets either more or less than any other. 'Every man to count for one and no one to count for more than one': this is the maxim that best sums up the idea of equality in the simple sense.[17] All modern societies try to apply it to the distribution of certain values, and the idea itself is very widely known. In traditional societies too it was acknowledged, but within restricted spheres, as for instance in the domain of kinship and, up to a point, of religion.

But beyond a certain point, a just distribution of values has to take differences between persons into account. Proportional equality consists in maintaining a just proportion while taking into account the differences among persons. If we accept that there are differences among persons and that different persons have to be treated differently, we can still apply the principle of equality, this time not in a simple sense, but by keeping some relevant criterion in mind. Here it is a question of classifying people, and giving every member of each class an equal right to what is allotted to the class as a whole.[18]

[16] Aristotle, *Politics* (trans. Jowett), Clarendon Press, p. 189; the Warrington edition has it thus: 'But equality is of two kinds—numerical and proportionate to desert. Numerical equality implies that one receives exactly the same (i.e. equivalent) number of things or volume of a thing as everyone else. Equality proportionate to desert implies treatment based on equality of ratios.' (Aristotle *Politics and the Athenian Constitution*, J. M. Dent, 1959, p. 135)

[17] See Berlin, 'Equality', p. 81 ff. The phrase is Jeremy Bentham's.

[18] Ibid. See also Bernard Williams, 'The Idea of Equality' in P. Laslett and W. G. Runciman (eds.), *Philosophy, Politics and Society*, second series, Basil Blackwell, 1962, pp. 110–31.

But the classification may be made according to merit or according to need, and the implications of the two from the point of view of distribution will be very different. While Aristotle paid much attention to merit, our modern commitment to welfare requires us to pay attention also to need. We know, or believe we know, that people differ according to merit, and if we allot equal rewards for equal merit, we are inclined to feel that the principle of equality has been in some sense satisfied. But people differ also according to need, and we might feel that real, as opposed to formal, equality can be achieved only if we make our distribution proportional to the needs of persons. The first of these two principles may be called the meritarian principle, and the second the compensatory principle. As we shall see, there are basic and fundamental tensions between the two, although both principles are invoked in the name of equality.

It would be a mistake to think that these distinctions are made only by professional philosophers or that they are only of academic value. We make them all the time, and, as such, it is important to ensure that we make them consistently and keep their implications clearly in mind. These are the very distinctions we find in Nehru's reflections on equality and inequality set down on the eve of Independence. When he wrote that 'the spirit of the age is in favour of equality' and that 'the spirit of the age will triumph',[19] he had in mind, first of all, the elimination of artificial barriers, such as those of caste, estate or race: this is equality in the simple sense.

But then Nehru went on to say, 'That does not and cannot mean that everybody is physically or intellectually or spiritually equal or can be made so. But it does mean equal opportunites for all and no political, economic or social barrier in the way of any individual or group';[20] or, in other words, reward must bear some proportion to ability, merit or talent. Nor is this all: for 'not only must equal opportunities be given to all, but special opportunities for educational, economic and cultural growth must be given to backward groups so as to enable them to catch up to those who are ahead of them';[21] which is to say that there must be compensation for need and not just reward for merit.

To say that the spirit of the age is in favour of equality is not to say that there are no critics of egalitarianism, either in this country

---

[19] J. Nehru, *The Discovery of India*, Asia Publishing House, 1961, p. 521.
[20] Ibid.   [21] Ibid.

or in the West. There are critics of egalitarianism among scholars as well as men in public life. The most obvious target of attack is what I have described as equality in the simple sense. It can be made to appear absurd by showing that nobody would seriously wish everyone to be treated equally in all respects. Or, it can be made to appear vacuous by showing that so many qualifications have to be made in order to take differences between persons into account that eventually very little content remains in the maxim, 'everyone is to count for one, and no one is to count for more than one'.

A few years ago J. R. Lucas, an Oxford philosopher, wrote an article entitled 'Against Equality' in which he attacked the positions adopted by the egalitarians, and concluded, 'The central argument for Equality is a muddle.'[22] The argument advanced by Lucas himself is purely formal and pays no attention to the social and historical conditions under which men and women strive to attain equality. More recently a prominent member of the British cabinet, Sir Keith Joseph, has co-authored a book in which he restates the nineteenth-century argument that, since human beings are by nature unequal, it is both futile and perverse to try to establish a social order on the basis of equality.[23]

A strong argument in favour of equality is that equal distribution does not call for any specific justification, whereas any unequal distribution, being but a particular case of unequal distribution, does. Isaiah Berlin puts it thus: 'If I have a cake and there are ten persons among whom I wish to divide it, then if I give exactly one tenth to each, this will not, at any rate automatically, call for justification; whereas if I depart from this principle of equal division I am expected to produce a special reason.'[24] This is not to argue that good reasons can never be found for unequal division. It is only to suggest that what are offered as reasons are not always good reasons but often specious ones, as for example that men should receive more education than women because they have superior intelligence.

Thus, there is a great deal to be said in favour of the idea of simple equality, with all its limitations. The value we place on it can be illustrated by the commitment in our Constitution to the principle of adult suffrage: every citizen, subject to a certain qualification of age, which every citizen is expected to meet in the ordinary course, has an equal right to elect representatives to Parliament and to the state

---

[22] J. R. Lucas, 'Against Equality', *Philosophy*, October 1965, pp. 296–307.

[23] K. Joseph and J. Sumption, *Equality*, John Murray, 1979.

[24] Berlin, 'Equality', p. 84.

Assemblies (Art. 326). Now that we have this right, we tend to take it for granted, and perhaps also to abuse it. But we have only to turn to our own recent history, or indeed, to some of our neighbouring countries today to realize that equality in even this simple sense means something, and that people have had to fight in order to achieve it.

If we go back only a couple of hundred years in time we will realize how novel, in historical terms, the very idea of full adult franchise is. The Levellers became famous as an ultra-Republican sect or movement whose leaders supported the people's cause in mid-seventeenth century England. But, as a recent student of that period pointed out, 'the Levellers consistently excluded from their franchise proposals two substantial categories of men, namely servants or wage earners, and those in receipt of alms or beggars.'[25] And there was no question of extending the franchise to women. Today it requires some effort to see such a movement as a people's movement.

The very idea of citizenship entails an element of equality—equality in the simple sense—that we tend to take for granted because we tend to take citizenship itself for granted. And yet, the right of citizenship—along with 'equality before the law' and 'the equal protection of the laws'—is not something that all Indians have always enjoyed. I know that there are still villages in India where Untouchables do not have the status of full members. If we condemn this violation of our laws regarding citizenship, how much more must we condemn the laws themselves which required that 'the dwellings of Chandalas and Shvapachas shall be outside the village . . . their dress the garments of the dead . . . their food . . . given to them . . . in a broken dish'.

It is not difficult to find the rationale behind the idea of simple equality—citizenship, equality before the law, equal protection of the laws—and we have to consider it, however briefly. There are undoubtedly differences between persons, and there have to be differences of treatment. From here one might be inclined to argue that

[25] C. B. Macpherson, *The Political Theory of Possessive Individualism*, Oxford University Press, 1964, p. 107. Macpherson adds, 'The term servant in seventeenth-century England meant anyone who worked for an employer for wages, whether the wages were by piece-rates or time-rates, and whether hired by the day or week or by the year' (p. 282), and shows that servants and alms-takers constituted a very substantial part of the population. For a somewhat different point of view based on a consideration of other material, see Christopher Hill, *The World Turned Upside Down*, Temple Smith, 1972.

for every difference between persons there ought to be a difference of treatment. It is this argument that we must categorically reject as being contrary to both reason and morality. The idea of simple equality merely suggests that differences between persons need not entail differences of treatment; and we can give substance to it only to the extent that we strive to extend those areas of life in which differences between persons are not allowed to interfere with our treatment of them as equal human beings.

To treat people alike, irrespective of outward differences, is to treat them from the human point of view as against the point of view of race, or of caste or of gender. What is meant by treating people from the human point of view can perhaps be best brought home by considering an example of the denial of such treatment. The example I have in mind is the attempt to justify the ill treatment of slaves in the New World by the argument that slaves, being Blacks, were not human beings in the full sense of the term.[26] Another example is the omission of the Aborigines from the censuses of population conducted in Australia until recently; they simply did not count as human beings.[27] These are extreme examples, but in a country which has been under colonial rule for two centuries it should not be difficult for even the privileged to understand what denial of consideration from the human point of view might signify.

The case for the human point of view in the context of equality has recently been eloquently made by the English philosopher Bernard Williams, and I cannot do better than to refer to his argument here. Williams first draws attention to certain common human capacities, and then goes on to show how important it is to keep these in mind while making an assessment of any kind of social arrangement:

> The assertion that men are alike in the possession of these characteristics is, while indisputable and (it may be) even necessarily true, not trivial. For it is certain that there are political and social arrangements that systematically neglect these characteristics in the case of some groups of men, while being fully aware of them in

[26] The most comprehensive modern study is G. Myrdal, *An American Dilemma*, Harper, 1944, of which Chapter 4, 'Racial Beliefs', is of special interest here. A classic account is to be found in Tocqueville, *Democracy in America*, vol. 1, chapter 18, 'The Present and Probable Future Condition of the Three Races that Inhabit the Territory of the United States'.

[27] F. L. Jones, *The Structure and Growth of Australia's Aboriginal Population*, Australian National University Press, 1970.

the case of others; that is to say, they treat certain men as though they did not possess these characteristics, and neglect moral claims that arise from these characteristics and which would be admitted to arise from them.[28]

He goes on to add that differences of treatment must rest on some moral principle and not merely on an arbitrary assertion of will.

A student of comparative sociology should hesitate to characterize the arrangements in any society or the reasons offered for such arrangements as arbitrary. At the same time, we cannot but be struck by the nature and number of invidious distinctions recognized and endorsed by the guardians of the traditional legal order in India. No society has allowed such a luxuriant growth of invidious social distinctions as ours. These distinctions of caste, subcaste, sect, sub-sect and the like have acted over the centuries to smother, if not to efface, the human point of view.

We have to take special care in our consideration of the Backward Classes to keep the human point of view in the forefront. Few groups in history could have suffered from the denial of the human point of view as much or as long as they did. Nor is this all a matter of past history. For two thousand years Untouchables and Tribals have been treated as if they were less than human beings, and this treatment was justified by the argument that they and their children were in their capacities inherently inferior to those born to a superior station in life. These historical disabilities must be kept in mind in any consideration of equality in the new social order.

Principles of proportional equality seek to reconcile the demands of equality with inequalities that are already in existence. As such, they are more complex than the simple equality with which we have been so far concerned. It might be said that in dealing with proportional equality, whether in the context of merit or in the context of need, we are dealing not so much with equality in the strict sense as with justice, or, at best, with equity. But that would be to take too narrow a view of the matter, for the notion of equality must comprehend equality of opportunity and not merely equality of status.

To adopt the human point of view is not to deny or disregard the differences that exist among individuals. If we consider human beings in any real society, we will find all kinds of differences to exist among

[28] Williams, 'The Idea of Equality', p. 112.

them. There are differences that follow from their arrangement in a given social order. There are perhaps also differences that exist independently of this arrangement. For many people the basic and fundamental question is whether there is any correspondence between these two sets of differences.[29]

If we admit that there are differences in capacity and if we accept that there should be differences in reward, then in those matters where these differences are considered relevant, we should ensure a correspondence between the two. I believe that it was Aristotle who argued that to treat equals unequally is unjust, but that to treat unequals equally is also unjust.[30] Although Aristotle was by no means an ardent egalitarian, this particular formulation of the issue would be acceptable as reasonable to most. To take a trivial example, while it would be considered fair to distribute pieces of cake equally among students in a class, it might not be considered fair to distribute marks equally among them.

Every society is characterized by a certain division of labour through which the various activities necessary for collective existence are carried out in an organized manner. From the sociological point of view the division of labour is in some sense what provides each society with its defining features. For example, the division of labour in a traditional Indian village, based on the *jajmani* system, is radically different from what we find in a modern industrial town. The tasks to be performed are different, there are differences in degrees of specialization, and the number of roles and their mutual connections also differ. The division of labour is most clearly manifested in the economic order, particularly in the occupational system, although in a broad sense it may be taken to cover society as a whole.

There are sharp differences of opinion among social theorists about the nature and significance of the division of labour. The French sociologist, Émile Durkheim, took on the whole a positive view of it. Writing in the last decade of the nineteenth century, he noted first and foremost the tremendous expansion of the division of labour since the beginning of the industrial revolution.[31] New

---

[29] This is in a way the central question posed by Rousseau; see J.-J. Rousseau, 'A Discourse on the Origins of Inequality' in *The Social Contract and Other Essays*, Dent, 1938. See also my Auguste Comte Memorial Lecture, 1979, *The Idea of Natural Inequality*, republished in this volume, pp. 7–32.

[30] Aristotle, *Ethics*, Penguin, 1978.

[31] É. Durkheim, *The Division of Labour in Society*, The Free Press, 1933.

occupations had emerged, and old ones had become divided and subdivided into various specialisms. The division of labour was not confined to the industrial field alone, but permeated every area of life, including the arts and the sciences. Durkheim argued that this was a welcome trend, because the division of labour not only brought material progress but also led to increased social cohesion, although he recognized that there were abnormal forms of it which were socially disruptive.

Marx, by contrast, took a very critical view of the division of labour.[32] He saw a close relationship between the division of labour on the one hand, and the capitalist system and commodity production on the other. Marx and Engels regarded the division of labour to be neither desirable nor inevitable. They had a vision of a future society in which no individual would be tied down to a particular occupational role, and each individual would move freely from one occupation to another according to his choice. At the same time, Marx recognized that such a society could not be created directly or immediately out of the existing social order.[33]

The experience of the twentieth century has shown how difficult it is to do away with the division of labour, and I speak not only of the Soviet Union, but also of China. Taking our Constitution and our social structure together, the reasonable position would seem to be that it is not a question of doing away with the division of labour but of regulating it. We can neither attain our economic objectives nor operate our administrative machinery without a properly regulated division of labour. All this requires at the very least a set of rules for recruiting persons to various social positions and for ensuring appropriate rewards for them for the proper performance of their tasks.

To return to Durkheim, his argument is that if the division of labour is to contribute to social well-being, 'it is not sufficient . . . that each have his task; it is . . . necessary that his task be fitting to him'.[34] However, this objective is achieved only when we have what Durkheim calls a spontaneous division of labour; it is defeated when we have what he calls a forced division of labour. The forced division of labour is, according to Durkheim, a pathological form of it, but

[32] See, in particular, *Capital*, vol. 1; see also K. Marx and F. Engels, *The German Ideology*, Progress Publishers, 1968.

[33] K. Marx, *Critique of the Gotha Programme*, Progress Publishers, 1978.

[34] Durkheim, *Division of Labour*, p. 375.

one which is likely to be particularly common in societies such as ours.

There is a forced division of labour when external constraints prevent a proper matching of the capacities of individuals with the tasks they are required to perform. We may visualize, on the one hand, a distribution of social positions that together constitute the division of labour; and on the other, a distribution of capacities and talents among the individual members of society. There is perhaps no society which has achieved a perfect concord between the two, but a commitment to such concord is, in my view, a part of our Constitutional commitment to equality. At the same time, our traditional social structure presents a whole series of obstacles to its realization. Family, lineage, clan, caste, sect and gender are what count, rather than individual capacity, in determining which individual will occupy which position in society.

For centuries it has been believed that a man's social capacities were known from the caste or the lineage into which he was born, and that no further test was necessary to determine what these capacities were. And it was considered axiomatic that men and women had radically different capacities not only biologically but also socially. To some extent they did grow up to have different social capacities. But we know today that these differences were a consequence of erroneous beliefs and the artificial social arrangements that rested on them. If we believe that men and women, or Brahmins and Shudras, are born with unequal mental capacities, and if we make unequal provision for their socialization on the basis of this erroneous belief, they will naturally develop unequal capacities as adults.

The scope for equality is severely restricted when women, Shudras, and all kinds of persons are excluded from positions of respect and responsibility in society with no consideration whatsoever for their individual capacities. It is in this context that the principle of equal opportunity acquires its real significance. This principle is written into our Constitution, in its very Preamble as well as among the Fundamental Rights. As I understand it, Art. 16 simply means that no office is too high for any member of society, whether Shudra or Untouchable, so long as there is the ability. Furthermore, equality of opportunity would signify nothing without the concomitant belief that ability or merit or talent might be discovered in any quarter of society whatsoever.

The idea of careers open to talent was a new one that was introduced into Europe in the wake of the French Revolution. It was a revolutionary idea precisely because in the old regime careers were not open to talent, but were determined by birth. The need to throw careers open to talent cannot be too strongly emphasized in our society where status has been more firmly fixed by birth than in any other society at a comparable level of development. The obstacles to free and open competition are many: there are not only objective factors, such as lack of means, but also subjective factors, like lack of motivation, that are a consequence of centuries of organized discrimination.

Today the meritarian principle makes it possible for Untouchables and persons from other disprivileged groups to attain to the highest positions in society, and this is a considerable change from the past. At the same time, it has to be admitted that there is something paradoxical about the principle itself of equality of opportunity. For equality of opportunity demands at best free and open competition. This means that there can be equality only before the competition, but not after it. In other words, equality of opportunity can and does lead to inequality of result, and this must be a source of serious concern in any social order with a fundamental commitment to equality.

It is one thing to recommend equality of opportunity as a way of eliminating discrimination; it is quite another when equality of opportunity becomes only an excuse for relentless competition without any regard for those who lose out in the race. In the West the very people who welcomed the idea of careers open to talent have now begun to be dismayed by the prospects of meritocracy. The publication in 1958 of Michael Young's satirical book, *The Rise of the Meritocracy*,[35] struck a responsive chord in many, and some began to wonder whether a meritocratic society can accommodate the human point of view any better than an aristocratic one.

The difficulty of achieving equality of status solely through equal opportunity becomes abundantly clear in our kind of society where the privileged are also overwhelmingly successful in every kind of competition. The fact that the sons of Untouchable labourers generally do much worse in life than the sons of Brahmin civil servants does not prove anything at all about the merits of the parties concerned. What it proves is the difficulty, if not the impossibility, of fully equalizing the external conditions of competition. Indeed, the

[35] M. Young, *The Rise of the Meritocracy*, Thames and Hudson, 1958.

examination system as well as the job market favours those who start with better resources and better motivation, both of which are products of their superior position in society. Those who lack these need some compensation if there is to be any prospect of achieving substantive as opposed to merely formal equality.

The idea behind the meritarian principle is that society must remove all artificial barriers against free competition, and then leave each individual to find his proper place according to his merit or his deserts. The idea behind the compensatory principle is that society must intervene in order to ensure that the competition is fair, and not just free. The first seeks merely to remove discrimination, and takes little account of the unequal needs of individuals who are unequally placed. The second seeks to take needs into account, and, at the same time, to provide some cushion against the excesses of untempered competition.

The meritarian principle draws its strength from the notion of equality of opportunity, but this notion itself shows a different aspect when we turn from the ideal to the real conditions of competition. In his Rajendra Prasad Memorial Lectures, Justice Mathew had said, using the words of Tawney, 'In the final analysis, equality of opportunity is not simply a matter of legal equality. Its existence depends, not merely on the absence of disabilities, but on the presence of abilities.'[36] Where these abilities have been damaged or destroyed by the agency of known historical forces, society has an obligation to restore them to life.

It was in the nineteenth century that the meritarian principle came into its own, expressing as it did the spirit of liberal capitalism with its faith in competition and the free market. The compensatory principle has achieved recognition more recently. It owes its inspiration to socialist rather than to liberal thought, and it relies more on the state than on the market for achieving its objective. To the extent that our Constitution has drawn inspiration from both liberal and socialist ideals, both principles are present in it.

What I have designated, perhaps inadequately, as the compensatory principle is recognized under different names in different

---

[36] Reprinted in K. K. Mathew, *Democracy, Equality and Freedom* (ed. Upendra Baxi), Eastern Book Company (Lucknow), 1978, p. 230. For the original, see R. H. Tawney, *Equality*, fourth edition, Unwin Books, 1964, p. 103.

societies. In some East European countries like Poland it is acknowl-edged in the contrast made between the 'meritocratic' and the 'socialist' principles of remuneration. In India it is known as 'protec-tive discrimination' since it seeks to discriminate in favour of groups that had in the past been discriminated against. It has found a place even in a capitalist society like that of the United States under the rubric of 'affirmative action'. In all cases its objective is to bring about equality under unequal circumstances.

The thrust of the contrast between the two principles of propor-tionality is well brought out in a survey of educational policy in his own country made by a distinguished Polish sociologist:

> Unequal conditions of cultural life at home cause the unequal cultural development of children from different strata. Hence workers and peasants support the maintenance of a preferential system of access to institutions of higher education for their children, who are less intellectually developed. Given the limited number of educational places, these preferential principles dimi-nish the automatic chances of children of the intelligentsia to enter the spheres of higher education. Consequently, all principles of selection based upon the results of 'purely' meritocratic examina-tions are especially popular among the intelligentsia. But this in turn automatically reduces the chances of children from worker and peasant families.[37]

We see from the above that a choice between the two principles is not merely a matter of moral judgement; it also involves a conflict of interests.

Both the meritarian and the compensatory principles are to be found among the equality provisions in our Constitution. It seems to me that the primary emphasis in the equality provisions in the part on Fundamental Rights is on the removal of discrimination and the provision of equality of opportunity. The spirit of these provisions seems to be that the individual rather than the caste or the sect is the irreducible unit of society, and that each individual be considered according to his particular merit or capacity or ability. The emphasis in the part on the Directive Principles seems to be somewhat dif-ferent: here the state is to take into account the special needs of certain strata of society, and to make special provisions for equalizing

[37] W. Wesolowski, *Classes, Strata and Power*, Routledge and Kegan Paul, 1979, p. 133.

the unequal conditions obtaining among the different strata.

Perhaps I have overdrawn the contrast between the two parts of the Constitution. Art. 16 itself qualifies the equal opportunity provision by special provisions for backward classes of citizens, and similar provisions have been introduced into Art. 15 by amendment of the Constitution. Nevertheless, there is a difference in spirit between the two types of provision. The first seeks to give free play to merit, the second seeks to accommodate needs. Further, the difference is not simply a difference between merit and need, but between individual merit and the needs of groups or classes of citizens.

If the meritarian principle applies primarily to individuals and the compensatory principle to collectivities, then we have to decide what kinds of collectivities are deserving of special attention. This will depend in part on the structure of groups and classes in the society concerned; but it will depend also on the value assigned in that society to the individual as such. In the United States, the Blacks, and, possibly other ethnic groups, are candidates for affirmative action. In India the groups especially marked out for protective discrimination are the Untouchables and the Tribals. In Poland, in the example cited above, the beneficiaries of preferential treatment in the educational system appear to be peasants and workers.

The idea behind protective discrimination and affirmative action is that certain groups, certain castes or races have special claims on society that cannot be sacrificed altogether to the pursuit of individual excellence. At the same time, no society, least of all a modern society in the second half of the twentieth century, can prosper unless it gives an important place to the claims of individual merit. For no matter which community we take and no matter how disprivileged it is, there will be rival claims to whatever it is that is allotted to it to meet its special needs; and it is difficult to see how individual merit can be overlooked altogether in settling rival claims among the individual members of any disprivileged community.

The compensatory principle, as I have labelled it, seeks to articulate a variety of sentiments. It rests on a recognition of existing social disparities as well as their historical basis. Its recognition of existing social disparities is reflected in its concern for the greater needs of some social strata as compared to others. But there is more to it than just this; there is also a sense of making reparation for ancient wrongs, of compensating whole groups and classes for the injuries they have suffered in the past. It is my belief that protective discrimination can and should seek to satisfy present needs; it can do nothing to repair past injuries.

It will not do to exaggerate either the limitations of the meritarian principle or the resources of the compensatory principle by narrowly linking the former with capitalism and the latter with socialism. It is true that historically the strong emphasis on individual merit has been associated with competition, laissez-faire and the free market, in short, with nineteenth-century capitalism; whereas the preoccupation with collective needs, social welfare and the protection of the weak have been associated with twentieth-century socialism. At the same time, no modern society, whether 'capitalist' or 'socialist' can afford to dispense with either principle and rely solely on the other. Even under socialism the educational system and the occupational system must give some place to individual merit as revealed by some form of competition; and even the most aggressively capitalist system has to give the state some role today in protecting the weak by means of compensatory action.

Our hesitation to leave everything to individual merit has grown with our distrust of untempered competition and the market principle. We have grown to value the welfare of the collectivity, and we have learnt that some intervention by society is necessary if that is to be achieved. But we must learn also to set limits to this intervention and to see that it does not become merely an euphemism for interference by the state and its bureaucracy. If the weakness of the meritarian principle was that it left too much to the hazards of the market, the weakness of the compensatory principle is that it tends to leave too much to official patronage. It is thus not a question of choosing between the meritarian and the compensatory principles, but of achieving a proper balance between the two.

We come back to the argument that the idea of equality is not a simple or a homogeneous one. There are different components to it, and it is not just a question of reconciling them in the abstract by means of some general formula. No society starts on a clean slate; every society has its own historical legacy. Age-old disparities must be taken into account if the equality in the new social order is to be real and not merely formal. At the same time, we must ensure that in destroying old inequalities we do not create new ones. Discrimination is a dangerous instrument, no matter how pure the intentions are of those who use it. Our own history ought to teach us how infectious the use of discrimination can be, and how careful we have to be in using it even for a desirable end.

These issues came up again and again when what is now Art. 16 was being debated in the Constituent Assembly more than thirty years ago, and I can do no better than to conclude by drawing attention to the observations made by Dr Ambedkar on that occasion. He drew attention to the different points of view that needed to be reconciled. There was first the general opinion 'that there shall be equality of opportunity for all citizens'. There was also the view that 'if this principle is to be operative . . . there ought to be no reservation of any sort for any class or community at all'. Then there was the opinion that 'although theoretically it is good to have the principle that there shall be equality of opportunity, there must at the same time be a provision made for the entry of certain communities which have so far been outside the administration.'[38]

What I find most appealing in Dr Ambedkar's own approach to the problem is its reasonableness and its freedom from dogmatism. He insisted on the need to take into account the special claims of certain communities which had for centuries been excluded from positions of respect and responsibility. At the same time, he warned against the possibility that these special claims might 'eat up' the general rule of equality of opportunity altogether. In his own words, 'we have to safeguard two things, namely, the principle of equality of opportunity and at the same time satisfy the demand of communities which have not had so far representation in the State.'[39] It remains to be seen whether discrimination which has in the past been a source of so much evil can, by being turned around, be made a source of good in the future.

II

The last lecture was devoted to the argument that there can be different ways of conceiving of equality. Our Constitution itself provides ample support for this argument, requiring us to take merit as well as need into account, and seeking to articulate the human point of view. These ideas, which we now find increasingly difficult to re-

[38] *Constituent Assembly Debates: Official Report*, vol. VII, p. 701.
[39] Ibid., p. 702.

concile, were all incorporated precisely because the Constitution was written with a keen awareness of the complex pattern of inequalities actually present in Indian society.

Few will argue that equality in any real sense can be achieved by the sole application of the meritarian principle, without any attention being paid to the unequal needs of people. Indeed, the limitations of the meritarian principle taken by itself have become apparent to most people in the second half of the twentieth century. In no society are the disparities between the well- and the ill-favoured more conspicuous than in India, and no project for the attainment of equality can hope to succeed if it turns a blind eye to these disparities. It is in this context that the compensatory principle acquires saliency in India; there has to be some discrimination if the weak are to contend with the strong on anything like terms of equality.

The plea for giving all sections of society a fair chance rather than making merit the sole criterion was urged consistently in the Constituent Assembly debates on the equality provisions. One of the Harijan members said: 'The Government can expect necessary qualifications or personality from the Harijans, but not merit. If you take merit alone into account, the Harijans cannot move forward.[40] Other members spoke about the special needs of the Harijans as a whole, and the various measures that might be adopted to meet them.

Earlier, in dealing with the distinction between merit and need, we came upon another distinction which we then left implicit, but which we must now make explicit. This is the distinction between the individual and the group. The two distinctions—between merit and need, and between the individual and the group—are not the same, but it is difficult to keep them apart in any discussion of equality, particularly in one concerned with protective discrimination. At this stage it is sufficient to say that the meritarian principle tends to take the individual alone into account, ignoring the group or community of which he might be a member. The compensatory principle, on the other hand, tends to identify the individual by the group or community to which he belongs, generally, though not invariably, by being born in it.

The policy of protective discrimination raises two issues which must both be kept in mind in any assessment we make of its successes and failures in India. There is, first of all, the question of how far we are going to reward merit, and how far make allowance for need.

[40] *Constituent Assembly Debates: Official Report*, vol. VII, p. 688.

There is also the question, equally important to my mind, of how we are going to balance the claims of the individual with those of the group or the community. We must view with caution a policy of protective discrimination which sets out to decrease the inequalities between castes and communities but ends by increasing the inequalities between individual members of each caste and community. It would be a mistake to believe that by making concessions to castes and communities we *automatically* satisfy the needs of all, or even the most deserving, of their individual members.

The application of the compensatory principle presupposes some kind of classification, and it has been well said in a Supreme Court judgement that 'discrimination is the essence of classification'.[41] The Constitution itself recognizes categories of individuals which it variously describes as the weaker sections or the backward classes. The Scheduled Tribes and the Scheduled Castes have been specified and listed. But there are also other classes or sections which appear to have special claims on the resources of the state either in return for past injuries or on account of present needs. It is impossible to assess these claims without a detailed examination of the structure of Indian society, the various communities, classes and sections of which it is composed, and their mutual relations.

It is easy enough to concede that not merit alone, but need also should be taken into account in the allocation of scarce resources. But there can be competing claims on the same resources, all on the basis of need. Take for instance the claims that might be made to services and posts on grounds of the special needs of individuals and classes: it would be disingenuous to pretend that there is no problem here of balancing the needs of various kinds of persons in meeting such claims. Critics of the meritocracy say, with some justice, that merit is an elusive thing, and that there is an arbitrary element in all judgements of merit. But we must not assume that we all know who has what needs, or that it is always easier to determine the relative needs of persons than it is to determine their relative merits.

The point has to be made at the outset that there are different kinds of needs as well as different ways of meeting them. There are some needs which may be met in such a way that rival claims do not arise, at least not in a direct or obvious way. For instance, one can think of whole sections of society standing in special need of primary education or basic medical care. If these are provided free of charge

[41] Ray, C. J. in State of Kerala *vs* N. M. Thomas (*A.I.R. 1976 S.C.* 497).

then the needs of those who cannot afford to pay for them are met without any damage to the claims in these regards of those who can afford to pay.

There are, however, other needs which cannot be met without some judgement being made on the merits of the rival claims. Where the opportunities for employment are few and there are many in need of employment, the claims of some individuals have to be sacrificed in order to meet those of others. This brings out a paradox inherent in the process of discrimination itself. For there is all the difference in the world between a form of protective discrimination from which a disprivileged community, class or section as a whole benefits, and one from which only a few of its individual members benefit. A great deal of what passes for protective discrimination or affirmative action is in fact of the latter rather than the former kind.

If it is true that 'discrimination is the essence of classification' then a great deal will hinge around the classification which determines who the weaker sections—or the backward classes—are. It would be a mistake to assume that such a classification is self-evident, or that it is given to us by the nature of things. It is true that in discussing inequality we often use a geological metaphor and speak of social stratification, as if the whole of society were divided into layers or strata, arranged one on top of another in the way in which the layers of the earth are arranged. But this is only a metaphor which can never do full justice to the complex and fluid patterns in which groups, classes and categories are arranged in a real human society.[42]

Some classifications seem to be organic or 'natural' because they have existed and been acknowledged for a very long time; such, for instance, is the classification of the Hindu population of India into its castes and subcastes. Other classifications appear to be 'rational' rather than natural because they are based on the kinds of impersonal criteria we feel ought to be used for making significant distinctions among people; such, for instance, is the classification of people according to their occupation. There obviously is some correspondence between the two, but a problem of choice arises where the correspondence ceases to obtain.

No society has only a single scheme of classification which it uses for every purpose; each has several such schemes among which one or a few may be more extensively used than the others. Broadly

[42] For a discussion of the distortions of the geological metaphor see A. Béteille, *Inequality among Men*, Basil Blackwell, 1977, chapter 6.

speaking, these schemes of classification are of two different kinds. The first uses the individual as its unit, and this gives us classes of individuals according to their income or occupation or education. The second uses the group as its unit, and this gives us an arrangement of clans or castes or other such groups, each having a kind of organic identity of its own. Many have been struck by the subordination of the individual to the group in our own traditional society. Nehru, for instance, described its structure thus: 'This structure was based on three concepts: the autonomous village community, caste, and the joint family system. In all these three it is the group that counts; the individual has a secondary place.'[43] These groupings, among which we shall be concerned primarily with castes, maintained an identity over and above that of their individual members, and perpetuated themselves by a kind of universal succession.

The distinction between societies which assign priority to the group in their classifications and those which assign priority to the individual corresponds in large measure to the distinction made famous by Henry Maine between societies based on status and those based on contract.[44] We have inherited a social order based on status, one in which the individual did not count for very much. 'Equality of opportunity' will mean very little if at every turn the individual is shadowed by the caste or the community into which he was born. Justice must be rendered to the castes and communities which have in the past been denied justice; but if we do this without any regard at all for the cost to the individual, instead of moving forward into the new social order promised by the makers of our Constitution, we might move backward into the Middle Ages.

Any discussion of the structure of Indian society must begin with a consideration of the inequalities that are to be encountered in almost every sphere of life. India has been viewed as a text-book example of a hierarchical society. If we take traditional institutions such as caste, village community and joint family, we will find that each is constituted according to a hierarchical design. The new

[43] J. Nehru, *The Discovery of India*, Asia Publishing House, 1961, pp. 247–8. See also N. K. Bose, *The Structure of Hindu Society*, Orient Longman, 1975; and L. Dumont, *Homo Hierarchicus: The Caste System and Its Implications*, Paladin, 1972.
[44] H. S. Maine, *Ancient Law*, Oxford University Press, 1950.

8

economic forces have not fully effaced this design, but have added other inequalities to those already in existence.

The most notable feature of inequality in Indian society from the past to the present is its visibility. Even though inequalities exist in all complex societies, they are in general more visible in agrarian as compared to industrial societies. Such inequalities are visible in the settlement pattern of our villages where the poor and the ill-favoured live apart from the rich and the well-born. Even in our large cities it is impossible not to be struck by the physical distinctions among people in their dress, appearance and deportment. Some of these distinctions are a consequence of widespread poverty; in a relatively affluent society there is a more even distribution of the basic amenities of life. But there are other distinctions that derive from the peculiarities of our traditional social order.

Social distinctions are not only more visible in India, they tend to be, on the whole, more rigid. By and large, individuals live and die in the station of life into which they are born; marriage also is fairly strictly regulated. There is little mobility, and the barriers between the classes and strata appear to be almost insurmountable. In a society in which the individual moves more or less freely from one level to another in the course of his life, his individual identity appears more important than the class or stratum to which he might belong at a particular moment. In a society characterized by immobility, on the other hand, an individual's personal qualities appear to be of less account than the group of which he is a part. This subordination of the individual to the group is a feature of our traditional social order to which we have already drawn attention; it is a feature that does not harmonize very easily with our new legal order.

Inequalities are not only visible and rigid, they are also highly elaborate. The social distance between the top and the bottom of the hierarchy is very large, and there are numerous grades in between. When we look at our traditional caste structure, we are struck by the divisions and subdivisions within it. When we look at our traditional agrarian hierarchy, we are struck equally by the number of intermediaries that stood between the landlord and the tiller of the land. The proliferation of invidious distinctions is a feature also of our modern social life. It has been said that many of these new distinctions are an artefact of colonial rule; even so, colonial rule found in our society a particularly fertile soil for generating distinctions of rank.

How are we to account for these inequalities whose existence is acknowledged by everyone? When and how did they originate, and what has sustained them over the centuries? Opinion is sharply divided on the question of the key to the problem of Indian inequality, and one may well ask whether there is in fact a single key to it. I shall consider two alternative approaches to the problem, because they indicate two different ways of identifying those who are most in need of special assistance.

For some people, the key to the problem of social inequality lies in the domain of material factors. They would say that there is pervasive inequality in India because of its all-round poverty, its general economic backwardness, and its slow rate of economic growth. Extremes of wealth and poverty are characteristic features of economically backward societies. A high rate of economic growth, on the other hand, creates the kinds of opportunities through which the barriers between classes and between strata become dissolved. A stagnant agrarian economy, long under colonial domination, has had very little scope for the loosening of its social rigidities.

The argument about the linkage between economic backwardness and social inequality has been made in a broad comparative and historical perspective by Gunnar Myrdal.[45] Myrdal contrasts the economically-backward societies of Asia with the economically-advanced societies of the West, and finds that, while inequalities exist in both, they are more visible, more rigid and more elaborate in the former than in the latter. Whether we attribute India's economic backwardness to its traditional institutional structure or to its prolonged subjection to colonial rule, there is no denying the fact that this backwardness has contributed much to the creation and maintenance of a very rigid system of social inequality.

The same contrasts are revealed when we examine the relationship between economic development and social inequality in a historical perspective. Western societies were not always characterized by high rates of economic growth. Pre-industrial society in Europe was, compared to the present, economically backward, and with this

[45] G. Myrdal, 'Chairman's Introduction' in A. de Reuck and J. Knight (eds.), *Caste and Race: Comparative Approaches*, J. & A. Churchill, 1967, pp. 1–4; see also his *Asian Drama: An Inquiry into the Poverty of Nations*, Penguin, 1968.

backwardness was associated the existence of all kinds of invidious social distinctions, although it is perhaps true that neither the degree of economic backwardness nor the extent of social inequality there was ever as great as in India. With the creation of new economic opportunities in the West, many of the traditional social distinctions began to dissolve, and a fairly fluid system of classes came to replace the more rigid system of estates characteristic of the past.

Those who assign primacy to the economic dimension of social inequality tend to view the problem of backwardness in India as being different only in degree from similar problems elsewhere. Perhaps the extent of poverty is greater in this country than in other countries; perhaps more people, in both relative and absolute terms, are in need of special economic assistance here than elsewhere. From the viewpoint of the planner and the policy maker there would appear to be certain advantages in defining backwardness in purely economic terms; one can then measure its extent, and apply uniform rules for deciding how assistance may be matched with need in every individual instance.

But not everybody regards the problem of social inequality in India to be basically an economic problem. There are those who maintain that if we are to get to the root of inequality in India we must begin with what is unique to Indian society and not with what it has in common with other societies. They point out that disparities of wealth and income exist in all complex societies, whereas untouchability exists only in India, and that unless we understand the social basis of untouchability we will never be able to find a solution to the problem of backwardness in India. In this view poverty, and even destitution, is only an aspect of a larger problem which has its roots in the very structure of traditional Hindu society.[46]

Nobody can deny the special significance of the caste system for the problem of inequality in India, including contemporary India. From the sociological point of view, the caste system has a morphological aspect and an ideological aspect, and to a large extent the one has reinforced the other. Morphologically, the whole of Hindu society has been divided and subdivided into a large number of small and well-defined groups, ranked in an elaborate and complex hierarchy; it was these groups, rather than individuals, which constituted the building blocks of caste society. Ideologically, there has

---

[46] The sharpest recent statement of this point of view is to be found in Dumont, *Homo Hierarchicus*.

been a strong emphasis on collective as opposed to individual identity, and on hierarchy, particularly as viewed in terms of the opposition between purity and pollution; social superiority was defined not so much in terms of wealth as of purity, and the stigma of pollution rather than poverty was what defined social inferiority.

Indian society may be represented in terms of either its class structure or its caste structure. Each provides or at least claims to provide a kind of global perspective on Indian society. Those who advocate the perspective of class seek to explain by it not only inequality in its various forms but every other important aspect of life as well, from politics to religion. Alternatively, those who favour the perspective of caste argue that caste permeates every sphere of collective life in both its morphological and ideological aspects.

Sociologists who believe that caste provides the ground plan of Indian society maintain that 'class' is a category of capitalist society, or industrial society, or Western society, and that Indians themselves do not perceive their social world as being divided into classes as Europeans or Americans might do; one variant of this argument is that in India 'class' is nothing but a particular grouping of castes. The argument on the other side is that the perspective of caste is a backward-looking perspective on Indian society, that caste might have been significant in the past, but that today it is merely a shell that conceals the real cleavages in Indian society, which are those of class.

I believe the question to be of such fundamental importance to the application of what I have called the compensatory principle that I would like to devote some attention to it, however briefly. There are two obstacles to a clear understanding of the distinction between caste and class. Firstly, there is no general agreement as to what people mean by class, and, to some extent, even caste. Secondly, there is considerable correlation at the empirical level between caste and class, which inclines people to the somewhat misleading conclusion that caste is an aspect of class, or vice versa.

The distinction between caste and class, it appears to me, is drawn differently in the legal as against the sociological literature. The main reason behind this is that the lawyer tends to think of 'class' in a rather different way from the social scientist. Being a sociologist, I will not presume to make a judgement on these divergent conceptions of class. At the same time, important decisions of the Supreme Court refer to the sociological factors that are to be taken into account in defining the Backward Classes, and this encourages me to confront the legal with the sociological conception of class.

From the sociological point of view the legal conception of class appears to be very broad and very general. For the lawyer, class is a 'logical' rather than a 'sociological' category. In this sense a class is a category that we get by any kind of logically consistent classification. Clearly there is a sense in which we can talk about classes of numbers in mathematics, or of classes of phonemes in linguistics. The lawyer speaks of 'classes' of persons, and he is satisfied so long as the classification is reasonable in terms of the objective behind a particular Constitutional principle or legislative enactment. From his point of view it makes sense to describe as classes not only landowners, tenants and labourers, or upper-, middle- and lower-income groups, but also Tribals, Untouchables and other groups of castes and communities defined in a particular way for a particular object.

The sociologist tries to give a more restricted meaning to the concept of class.[47] He does not regard landowner, tenant and labourer on the one hand, and Brahmin, Jat and Chamar on the other, as being categories of the same kind. For him only the former constitute classes in the true sense of the term, and not the latter. The fact that most Chamars are agricultural labourers or that most Jats are cultivators does not make them into classes, for the identity of the first set of categories has a different basis from that of the second.

It is far from my intention to suggest that sociologists themselves are in complete agreement on the meaning of class. There is, first of all, the well-known difference of approach between Marxist and non-Marxist sociologists.[48] The Marxists tend not only to assign overwhelming significance to class, but also to define it in a particular way. Non-Marxists are, on the whole, more eclectic in the choice of criteria for defining class. I think it would be fair to say that sociologists are more in agreement on what should not be reckoned as class than on what class actually is.

[47] Sometimes the social anthropologist also uses the wider conception of class, as, for instance, in talking about marriage 'classes' among the Australian aborigines. But this usage is today acknowledged to be archaic, if not eccentric. See C. Lévi-Strauss, *The Elementary Structures of Kinship*, Alden Press, 1969.

[48] For a discussion of various conceptions of class (and of 'classlessness'), see S. Ossowski, *Class Structure in the Social Consciousness*, Routledge and Kegan Paul, 1963.

There are two interrelated components to what may be considered as the common core of the sociological conception of class. The first relates to the kinds of criteria by which classes are differentiated from each other, and the second to the kinds of units with which classes are constructed by the application of such criteria. The criteria used for differentiating classes are economic criteria, and classes are made up of individuals who have only their economic conditions in common. The importance of the economic criterion in the definition of classes will be readily acknowledged. The significance of starting with the individual in reckoning classes is less easily recognized; it becomes manifest only when we contrast a system of classes with a system of castes.

It is not enough to say that social classes should be defined by economic criteria, because one can think of several economic criteria which are not all of the same kind. Here again the Marxist viewpoint is distinctive because it insists that, objectively, classes should be defined in terms of the sole criterion of the ownership or non-ownership of the means of production. But others have pointed to the independent importance of occupation and income.[49] Among those who own no land or capital there may be some who are in superior occupations and earn high incomes; conversely, some property owners may have smaller incomes and lower prestige than some individuals in high-salaried occupations who may not own any property at all. At any rate, nobody can deny that in the contemporary world an individual's income and occupation—and perhaps also his education—are good indicators of his needs, and of his capacity to meet the needs of the members of his household.

Whichever way we look at it, a class is an aggregate of individuals (or, at best, of households), and, as such, quite different from a caste which is an enduring group. The distinction between an aggregate of individuals and an enduring group is of fundamental significance to the sociologist, and, I suspect, to the jurist as well.[50] A class derives the character it has by virtue of the characteristics of its individual members. In the case of caste, on the other hand, it is the group that stamps the individual with its own characteristics.

[49] See, for instance, G. D. H. Cole, *Studies in Class Structure*, Routledge and Kegan Paul, 1955.

[50] Some sociologists draw their support for the distinction from the legal literature. See, for instance, M. Fortes, *Kinship and the Social Order*, Routledge and Kegan Paul, 1970, chapter XIV.

There are some affiliations which an individual may change, including that of his class; he cannot change his caste. At least in principle a caste remains the same caste even when a majority of its individual members change their occupation, or their income, or even their relation to the means of production; it would be absurd from the sociological point of view to think of a class in this way. A caste is a grouping *sui generis*, very different from a class, particularly when we define class in terms of income or occupation.

The irreducible identity of castes in Indian society is acknowledged by sociologists as well as lawyers. I interpret Justice Hegde's statement in a Supreme Court judgement that 'A caste has always been recognized as a class'[51] to mean simply that the existence of castes must be acknowledged as a significant part of our social reality. Yet there is a certain uneasiness about this acknowledgement in view of our commitment to a casteless society. I see a trace of this uneasiness in the statement in another recent Supreme Court judgement that the Scheduled Castes 'are not a caste within the ordinary meaning of caste'.[52] It is as if we were forced to acknowledge the existence of castes, wishing at the same time that they were classes!

A sociologist unfamiliar with the intricacies of Indian social structure is likely to detect a certain anomaly between the title of Part XVI of the Constitution and the provisions actually made under its various articles. For, while the title speaks of 'Special Provisions Relating to Certain Classes', all the articles except one deal with the Scheduled Castes, the Scheduled Tribes and the Anglo-Indian community. Where references are made specifically to the backward classes, as in Art. 338 (3) or in Art. 340, it is not altogether clear that they are conceived of as being different in kind from the Scheduled Castes, the Scheduled Tribes and the Anglo-Indian community. Again, it is perhaps a characteristic of our predicament that, in our Constitution as well as in everyday life, when we say 'class', as often as not, we mean 'community'. Even where the spirit of the age wants us to attend to the individual, castes and communities are forced on our attention by our traditional social structure.

Some students of the Indian Constitution have argued that the

---

[51] Hegde, J. in A. Periakarupian *vs* State of Tamil Nadu (*A.I.R.* 1973 *S.C.* 2310).

[52] Ray, C. J. in State of Kerala *vs* N. M. Thomas (*A.I.R.* 1976 *S.C.* 501).

only reasonable classification in the Indian context is the classification into castes and communities. This point of view has recently been put forward most forcefully by L. G. Havanur as Chairman of the Karnataka Backward Classes Commission. He states in his Report that:

> Class is synonymous with caste or tribe, so far as Hindus are concerned.
>
> Class is synonymous with tribe, or racial group, so far as tribal communities are concerned.
>
> Class is synonymous with section or group so far as Muslim, Christian and other religious communities and denominations are concerned.[53]

This would seem to leave very little room in the new legal order for any mode of classification other than those inherited from the past.

Much as one may disapprove of the categorical manner in which Mr Havanur presents his case, one cannot ignore the wealth of legal, historical and sociological material he has presented in support of it. This material shows the salience of castes and communities not only in our ancient past but also in our more recent history. It is true that the traditional legal order emphasized the group at the expense of the individual; but there can be little doubt that this emphasis was given an additional edge by the manner in which the British transferred power to Indians after two centuries of colonial domination.

Mr Havanur has shown how from the very beginning the leaders of the Indian National Congress sought to articulate the demands of the various classes in Indian society, by which they meant Muslims, Christians, Sikhs, Parsis, Brahmins, Depressed Classes, etc. The term 'Backward Classes' began to acquire currency from around 1919, and to be used broadly to include the Depressed Classes, the Aboriginal Tribes and Other Backward Classes. 'The word *class*, besides being used in official and semi-official documents, was also being used by political leaders, social reformers and the like to apply to castes, tribes and communal groups.'[54] In the case of Muslims, Christians and Parsis there could be very little scope for confusing the loose meaning of 'class' with its strict socio-economic definition;

[53] Karnataka Backward Classes Commission (Chairman, L. G. Havanur), *Report*, Government of Karnataka, 1975, vol. 1, part I, pp. 98–9.

[54] Ibid., p. 58.

in the case of the Backward Classes some scope for such confusion obviously exists.

In the three decades preceding the formation of the Constituent Assembly the divisions into castes and communities that had existed in Indian society from ancient times acquired a new kind of legitimacy through the political process. Communal politics, minority politics and the politics of backwardness became closely intermeshed. It is in this light that we have to interpret Mr Havanur's laconic statement, 'Caste has come to stay'.[55] The British made their contribution to the crystallization of the political identities of castes and communities in the emerging social order. This was partly because they felt that they had a special responsibility in protecting the interests of the minorities and the Backward Classes in the competition for power. But it was also because the demand for self-government could be kept at bay by playing one community off against another.

The balance of power between castes and communities was an important concern for those who participated in the deliberations of the Constituent Assembly. The equality provisions that came to be written into the Constitution, particularly the provisions relating to protective discrimination, cannot be understood in isolation from this concern. Those to whom special provisions were to apply were at first conceived in a broad way, to include a variety of castes and communities; classes in the strict sense of the term hardly figured in this consideration. There were those who wanted the religious minorities to be included, and there were those who argued for the inclusion of virtually all Non-Brahmin Hindu castes. When Dr Ambedkar proposed that benefits be reserved for the backward classes, it was argued against him that if this was done and if the backward classes were defined in a limited and restricted manner, the special claims of millions of others would be overlooked.[56]

The special claims of the Scheduled Castes and the Scheduled Tribes arise out of the conditions under which they have been constrained to live from ancient times. The defining feature of their condition was that they were in many important regards placed *outside* the bounds of the larger society, the Scheduled Tribes on account of their isolation in particular ecological niches, and the

[55] Ibid., p. iii.
[56] *Constituent Assembly Debates: Official Report*, vol. VII, passim.

Scheduled Castes on account of the segregation imposed on them by the rules of pollution.[57] There were in the past, as there are at present, many different tribes among the Adivasis and many different castes among the Harijans, but they all shared in common the condition of being in one sense or another exterior to the larger society.

The exteriority of these two groups of communities puts their claims on a totally different level from the claims of all other communities in Indian society. Most of the disprivileges from which they have suffered and many of those from which they still suffer can in one way or another be related to it. So long as this condition exists the very possibility of creating equality in the external conditions of competition is denied.

It has to be emphasized that the disabilities from which the Harijans and the Adivasis suffered were in each case imposed on the community as a whole, and not on individual members of particular communities. This was notably so in regard to the stigma of pollution which was the lot of every Harijan caste in traditional Hindu society. P. V. Kane has brought out well the distinction between individual segregation and collective segregation on account of pollution.[58] The segregation of the individual, of no matter what caste, on account of the pollution of birth or death was temporary; quite different was the segregation of whole communities on account of a pollution that was imposed on them as a permanent and inescapable condition of life.

The isolation of the tribal communities was likewise a collective and not an individual affair. Its isolation enabled each tribal community to retain its own social organization, its own customs, its own religion and, above all, its own language. It also imposed on its members a rather low level of material existence. Indeed, what came to be identified as the tribal population of India in the nineteenth and twentieth centuries consisted precisely of those communities which by virtue of their material and cultural isolation had remained outside the mainstream of national life. Their collective deprivation has been in every way as marked as that of the Untouchables.

Although the deprivations traditionally suffered by the Harijans and the Adivasis were different in their specific manifestations, there is a certain logic in treating them together from the viewpoint of

[57] See my 'The Future of the Backward Classes' in A. Béteille, *Castes: Old and New*, Asia Publishing House, 1969.

[58] P. V. Kane, *History of Dharamasastra*, Bhandarkar Oriental Research Institute (Poona), 1974, vol. II, part I, pp. 168–70.

protective discrimination. Those who have been kept out require special facilities to be brought in. Special care has to be taken to ensure that they are able to exercise their rights as full citizens in the new legal order. Above all, no cost should be counted too high if it ensures the widest diffusion of literacy and education among them. Since disabilities have been imposed on entire communities, those measures should have the highest priority which directly benefit the largest number of individual members of these communities.

In a very broad sense each caste fixed its collective identity on its individual members and all castes had a position inferior to the Brahmins. Some such argument has been made to claim special concessions for a whole range of castes and communities which occupied the middle levels of the traditional ritual hierarchy. The implication of this is that our first priority ought to be to bring about equality between castes before we attempt to bring about equality between individuals. This, it seems to me, is the spirit behind Mr Havanur's somewhat unusual interpretation of the Constitution: 'Hence the Constitution suggests *recognition of castes for their equalisation.*'[59]

It would be wrong to argue that in providing for equal opportunity, or even the equalization of opportunities among those unequally placed, we should always give priority to the group over the individual. Such a course might be justified if all the groups with which we are concerned—castes and communities—were absolutely homogeneous on every significant scale of inequality. But we know perfectly well that they are not. Firstly, a caste which has a low ritual status may be materially well off; secondly, individual members of most castes vary considerably in their actual material condition, irrespective of the traditional ritual status of their caste. It is only at the very lowest end of the scale that the assumption of uniform deprivation holds true to a large extent.

The assumption of perfect congruence between the collective ritual status of a caste and the actual material condition of its individual members does not hold good today, and probably never held good in the majority of cases even in the past. Various forces are at work today which increase the dissociation between caste and income, caste and occupation, and caste and education. These forces draw the individual relentlessly away from the power and the protection of his caste. They compel us to take more and more account

[59] Karnataka Backward Classes Commission, *Report*, p. 36; emphasis in original.

of the needs of the individual irrespective of his caste, for his caste tells us less and less about the total range of his deprivations. The new legal order must make provision for the individual to bring his needs to the attention of the state in his own right, without the mediation of his caste.

To the understanding of a sociologist, the very concept of citizenship in the Constitution of India is that it is an unmediated relationship between the individual and the state. This is a modern concept, characteristic of societies of a particular kind, and not a universal feature of all human societies. The modern concept of unmediated citizenship may be contrasted with the pattern prevalent in traditional West African societies where, Meyer Fortes tells us, 'it is a fundamental principle of Ashanti law that lineage membership is an inextinguishable jural capacity and the basic credential for citizenship'.[60] It was much the same in traditional Hindu society: the individual was a member of society by virtue of his membership of a caste which he acquired by birth into a particular family.

Now it is one thing to make provisions of a specific nature and for a limited duration for the Scheduled Castes and Scheduled Tribes in order to protect them from injury and abuse, and in order to ensure that the conditions under which they compete with other members of society are fair and not just free. It is quite another thing to make the scope of protective discrimination so extensive that in every case, or in almost every case, the caste to which an individual belongs becomes a relevant factor in determining his entitlements. For the idea of citizenship as inscribed in our Constitution is the very antithesis of the traditional idea that caste membership 'is an inextinguishable jural capacity and the basic credential for citizenship'.

The meritarian principle, as I noted earlier, has been closely, and, no doubt rightly, associated with individualism, and we cannot ignore the many sins that have been laid at the door of individualism, especially by the advocates of socialism. But we cannot throw out individualism root and branch merely on account of its excesses or its perverse expressions. We may not share all of Durkheim's enthusiasm for individualism as the source of a new religion and a new morality,[61] but we must not hesitate to acknowledge what we

[60] Fortes, *Kinship and the Social Order*, p. 147.

[61] Durkheim's celebrated defence of individualism was made in the cause of Alfred Dreyfus. See É. Durkheim, 'Individualism and the Intellectuals' (trans. S. & J. Lukes) in *Political Studies*, vol. XVII, 1969, pp. 114–30.

owe to the individual. Above all, in the context of Indian society, here and now, we must realize that the alternative to individualism may not be the cherished dream of socialism, but a moral order in which the individual is once again displaced by clan, caste and community.

The shadow of the community loomed large over the minds of many of those who had assembled to prepare the Constitution. In particular, there was much sentimental attachment to the idea of the traditional village community. While presenting the Draft Constitution, Dr Ambedkar attacked the village community and said, 'I am glad that the Draft Constitution has discarded the village and adopted the individual as its unit.'[62] In the debate that followed many were vocal in the cause of the village, but few spoke up for the individual; and yet what they wrote down would signify little without the individual being given a place in the centre.

Those who view inequality in terms of the hierarchy of castes tend to emphasize ritual status, because it was this rather than income or wealth or even occupation that was fixed at the same level for all individual members of a caste. On the other hand, there are those who view inequality in economic terms, and they tend to emphasize the distribution of income and wealth among individuals. We now have a fairly large number of studies of poverty and income distribution which tend to present a somewhat different picture of inequality in Indian society from the one we have just been considering.[63] Unfortunately, there has been very little synthesis of the work done on inequality by sociologists whose emphasis is on the hierarchy of castes, and the work done by economists whose emphasis is on the distribution of income between individuals and between households.

However strongly one might feel about the rigidities of caste, it will generally be conceded that these are no longer as severe as they were even a generation ago. The stigma of pollution, the segregation of Untouchables and the isolation of Tribals persist in practice, no matter what the law lays down, but even the practice is less uniform

[62] *Constituent Assembly Debates: Official Report*, vol. VII, p. 39.

[63] V. M. Dandekar and N. Rath, *Poverty in India*, Indian School of Political Economy (Bombay), 1971; T. N. Srinivasan and P. K. Bardhan (eds.), *Poverty and Income Distribution in India*, Statistical Publishing Society (Calcutta), 1974.

and less rigid than in the past. The sense of distance between castes
considered superior and inferior has in general become attenuated;
at any rate, no sociologist will seriously argue that the social distance
between castes that was a part of the traditional order is now on the
increase. It is otherwise with economic inequality and poverty. The
absolute number of those below the poverty line is increasing, and
there is no clear evidence that their proportion in the population as
a whole is declining.

Whereas sociologists talk about the social backwardness of castes
and communities, economists emphasize the material poverty of
classes of individuals. The depth and extent of poverty, and the size
of the classes in its grip have received expert attention from economists only recently. There are enormous difficulties in arriving at
agreed measures of poverty in a country such as ours. Statistics on
income and expenditure are difficult to collect in a predominantly
agrarian economy, and where levels of living are so low, there is room
for disagreement among experts on where the line of poverty in an
absolute sense ought to be drawn. There is, however, general agreement that substantial sections of our population—anything between
25 and 40 per cent of the total—live under conditions of extreme
poverty.

Poverty no doubt existed in this country in the past as well, and
some of its roots clearly go back to the traditional social order. But
there are aspects of it that are equally clearly of more recent origin.
It is doubtful if India ever witnessed such a massive concentration of
poverty as one may see today in cities such as Calcutta, Bombay and
Madras. Properly speaking, these are neither industrial nor pre-
industrial cities; they owe their origin to the economic demands of
capitalist expansion under colonial dominance. It may be argued that
concentrated poverty has increased not only in the urban but also in
the rural areas, and similar forces have been responsible for their
increase in both cases.

The forces that lead to the concentration of poverty and the
increase of economic inequality between individuals are also the ones
that disrupt the traditional structure of castes and communities.
Capitalism creates new inequalities, but it also undermines old ones.
The economic forces that push people below the line of poverty do
not pay much regard to the finer points of the traditional distinctions
of status. Those who move into the slums of a large city leave behind
a part of their traditional identity, including their traditional con-

cerns for purity and pollution. The pavement dwellers of Calcutta include people from all castes and communities, though not in equal proportions; it would be unrealistic to believe that old distinctions can survive unchanged under these new conditions of life.

It has often been said that, despite its iniquities, the traditional order assured a measure of economic security to members of all castes, including the lowest. Each caste was assigned a specific occupation, and its members had a kind of hereditary right over that occupation. Economic relations were governed by status rather than contract, and the community as a whole had an obligation to see that all its members had some gainful employment. This is no longer the case either in principle or in practice. Employment is determined by the impersonal laws of the market which every year add to the number of unemployed individuals from every caste and community.[64] One's life chances, including one's employment prospects, are no longer guaranteed by caste, although they may be greatly improved by birth in a wealthy family of no matter what caste.

Traditionally the status of a caste was closely linked to the occupation over which its members had hereditary rights, but the nature of the relationship between caste and occupation has been much misrepresented. A caste occupation, properly speaking, is the occupation traditionally associated with the caste as a whole, and not the occupation actually practised by its individual members. It is doubtful that there was at any time a complete correspondence between the two. At any rate, even before Independence many castes, and probably most, had more than half their working members in occupations other than those specifically associated with their caste.[65]

It should be clear that even when one acknowledges the desirability of limiting the claims of merit by those of need, it is not easy to determine what kinds of needs there are and how they are to be met. It is one thing to try to satisfy needs through the provision of general facilities such as those relating to nutrition, health and literacy, and quite another to make special provisions, such as those relating to

[64] It is a noteworthy feature of sociological studies in India that they have paid hardly any attention to downward mobility as compared to the attention devoted to upward mobility. Again, this is partly because downward mobility is hardly visible any longer in the caste system, although it is very conspicuous in the class system.

[65] N. K. Bose had pointed this out in studies he had made in the forties. See Bose, *The Structure of Hindu Society*, chapter 11.

job reservation, that can satisfy directly only a few individual members of groups that are made up of very many. In particular it is fallacious to argue that the equalization of castes can be achieved by means of job reservations in the government. Such jobs are too few in number to materially alter the conditions of any caste as a whole; and there is little reason to believe that the personal advancement of an individual and the social betterment of the caste into which he was born have very much to do with each other.

In matters such as job reservation we have to consider seriously how much weightage to give to the material condition of the individual candidate and how much, if any, to the social status of the caste to which he belongs. Attempts have been made, as in the state of Kerala, to apply a means test in addition to the test of caste or community, but the result does not appear to have been materially different from what one might get by applying the caste test alone.[66] It is now becoming increasingly clear that in seeking to do justice to castes or communities we might deny justice to individuals, for we cannot any longer pretend that all or most or even many of the needs of the individual will automatically be taken care of by his caste, once the status of that caste is enhanced. The ends of justice are hardly met if our vain endeavour to bring about equality between castes leads only to the increase of inequality among the individual members of every caste.

Leaving aside the very special claims of the Scheduled Castes and the Scheduled Tribes, we have to concede that poverty is a very serious problem in Indian society, and that in choosing its victims it does not necessarily discriminate among castes. Justice Gajendragadkar's statement that social backwardness is 'the result of poverty to a very large extent'[67] is perhaps even more true today than when it was made nearly twenty years ago. More recently Jagjivan Ram has observed that 'Problems of a poor Brahmin and a poor Harijan are the same.'[68] Certainly the problems of a poor Brahmin may be more acute than those of a well-to-do member of a 'backward' caste demanding a place in the administration on the plea that his community has fewer than the average number of members in it.

To argue that a 'poor Brahmin and a poor Harijan' should be

[66] *Report of the Backward Classes Reservation Commission, Kerala, 1970*, Government of Kerala, 1971.
[67] *A.I.R. 1963 S.C.* 659.
[68] Reported in *The Statesman*, Delhi, 8 March 1980.

9

treated alike is to assert what I have earlier described as the human point of view. It is to maintain that considerations of race, caste and creed should be set aside when we are faced with the real needs of individual human beings. It is useful to remember that the human point of view may be asserted also on behalf of a Brahmin; and it is salutary to be reminded of this by a Harijan leader of national importance. In a caste-ridden society nothing is easier than to assert the human point of view on behalf of the members of one's own caste.

Clearly, in the case of the Untouchables, backwardness is not solely a matter of poverty, the extent of which might vary from one individual to another. It is due also to the stigma of pollution which attaches to the caste or community as a whole. Attitudes to pollution die hard in our society, and they reappear in the form of social prejudices which certainly weigh against the Untouchables, often heavily, in most competitive situations. The position of other castes which claim job reservation on a par with the Untouchables is hardly comparable. They cannot collectively claim to be victims of prejudice on account of their traditional status as Harijans and Adivasis can. In their case the particular circumstances of the individual claimants, rather than the status of the caste as a whole, must be considered decisive.

The prospects of material advancement through job reservation have led to a kind of competition for backwardness among castes at the middle levels of the hierarchy. This kind of competition creates a vested interest in backwardness, and it combines the worst features of a hierarchical and a free-market society. It stifles individual initiative without creating equality between individuals, and it obstructs the natural processes through which the barriers between castes and communities can be effaced. By making caste and community a relevant factor in every sphere of activity, it pushes the human point of view into the background.

The ideal of equality has at best a very insecure foothold in our society. It can never become securely established until we reject the distinctions of caste in all their implications. It is a mistake to separate completely the morphology of caste as a set of self-perpetuating groups from its ideology. The morphology and the ideology of caste are closely linked, and the ideology is totally antithetical to the values of equality. Thus, any effort to strengthen the identity of castes with a view to their equalization cannot but end in failure.

It is not true that the hierarchical values on which the distinctions of caste rest have never been challenged in Indian society before the modern age. It has often been pointed out that the first great protagonist of equality, the Buddha, was himself born in this land of hierarchy. Throughout the Middle Ages there was a succession of religious reform movements which challenged the established hierarchy of caste in the name of equality among men. But they all came to grief because of their inability to cut through the existing divisions of society. Describing the course of the movement for equality started by Chaitanya in eastern India, N. K. Bose wrote, 'The ideas propounded by Lord Chaitanya remained confined to particular sects; they were not able to break down the intolerance embedded in society as a whole and usher in a new flood of life. The Vaishnavas were in effect transformed into a new caste.'[69] This seems to have been the normal cycle of development: what started as a movement for social reform became hardened into a sect which became transformed into a caste which then found a place for itself in the established order of castes.

India has been described as the land of 'the most inviolable organization by birth',[70] and the subordination of the individual to the group is an inseparable aspect of this organization. It is here more than anywhere else that we have to be vigilant about claims made by individuals on the strength of their birth in a particular group. This society made a terrible mistake in the past in believing that merit was an attribute not of individuals but of groups, that being born a Brahmin was in itself a mark of merit. We shall make the same kind of mistake if we act on the belief that need too is always, and not just in special cases, an attribute of groups rather than of individuals.

[69] Bose, *The Structure of Hindu Society*, p. 132.
[70] M. Weber, *The Religion of India*, The Free Press, 1958, p. 3.

The Pursuit of Equality and the Indian University

The Duhr Memorial Lecture, 1980

Our contemporary life is permeated by the contradiction between the principle of equality and the practice of inequality. This contradiction is particularly marked in India where a Constitution with a strong emphasis on equality confronts the most bewildering variety of inequalities in almost every sphere of life. But it is not confined only to India; it is a feature of the whole modern world where the social reality falls very far short of the egalitarian spirit of the age. It was not always like this: in the past, particularly in India, a hierarchical order was more easily accepted by people, or at least it lay less heavily on their conscience.

I would like to examine the place of the university in contemporary Indian life in the light of the contradiction between the hierarchical social order inherited from the past and the present commitment to equality. We all expect the universities to reduce the constraints of hierarchy; but we also fear for their very survival against the rising tide of populist demands. Before we can determine what the universities can do to resolve the contradiction between the ideal of equality and the facts of inequality, we must see how they themselves get caught up in it.

The universities have come to occupy a large and, in my view, a permanent place in Indian life, although academics like to talk about their being in the grip of crisis. There certainly is an appearance of crisis on the university campus in almost every part of the country, if not an administrative or a financial crisis, then at least a political one. A crisis in a university receives more than its due share of public attention since university teachers and students in India, as elsewhere, are articulate if not reflective persons. As universities have grown in size, first students and then teachers have become unionized throughout the country. The demand for equality in the universities is not simply a matter of what is required by the free and unfettered pursuit of knowledge; it has to be seen also in terms of what is required by the government which finances them and by the unions which can decide whether they remain closed or open.

The Indian university is not characteristically a quiet place, tucked away in a remote corner. It has been from the very beginning associated with the metropolis. Further, universities have been established largely on the initiative of government, first the colonial government and then, after independence, the central and state governments. The first three universities were set up in 1857 at Calcutta, Bombay and Madras which were the principal centres of British rule in India. Between then and 1947, when the country became independent, the universities grew at a modest rate, but since then the expansion has been rapid. There were 19 universities in 1947 and there are now 108 universities with a total enrolment of over 2.5 million students.

The sixties was the decade of the greatest expansion of university education in India. Some forty new universities were added and the student enrolment grew at an average annual rate of 14 per cent. The rate of growth slowed down in the seventies when 29 new universities, several of them agricultural universities of small size, were added and student enrolment grew at an annual rate of only 4 per cent.[1] Given the enormous significance of demographic pressures in Indian society, this decline in the rate of growth might indicate the beginning of a new trend in the life of the Indian university. It is too early to speak with any confidence about such a trend because some of the change is notional, being the result of a shift in the cut-off point between secondary education and higher education.

Despite attempts by the University Grants Commission to ensure uniformity in matters ranging from teaching standards to salary scales, Indian universities in fact differ enormously in size, territorial jurisdiction, and material and intellectual resources. The three older universities are notoriously large in size, the oldest of them, the University of Calcutta, being also the largest with a total enrolment of over 150,000 students. Others, such as Aligarh Muslim University with 13,094, Jawaharlal Nehru University with 3,781 and Visva-Bharati with 1,453 students, are of medium or even small size.[2] The

[1] University Grants Commission, *Report for the Year 1979-80*, U.G.C. (New Delhi), n.d., p. 10.   [2] Ibid., Appendix I.

smaller universities tend to be residential whereas the larger ones can provide accommodation to only a small fraction of the student body.

Whether a university is small or large depends much on whether it is of the unitary or the affiliating type. In the former the university undertakes directly to enrol, accommodate and teach its students; in the latter a great deal of this is done through its affiliated colleges. In India the college came before the university, and without its colleges, the university could hardly cope with the pressure of students seeking its degrees. The unitary universities, which do without affiliated colleges, have smaller student bodies and are fewer in number, more than half of them being agricultural universities.

Most undergraduate teaching and a great deal of post-graduate teaching is done in the colleges rather than directly in the university departments. The affiliated colleges 'cater to 88.5 per cent of the total enrolment of students at the undergraduate level; 53.1 per cent at the postgraduate level and 14.0 per cent at the research level. Teachers employed in colleges constituted nearly 79 per cent of the total number of teachers in the universities and colleges during 1979–80.'[3] Thus, the very large size of the Indian university is in a way deceptive. At the undergraduate level, in the affiliating type of university, teaching is done separately in each affiliated college so that undergraduate classes are quite small even in a university like the University of Delhi which has a total enrolment of nearly 70,000 students.

There is between the college and the university department not only a division of functions but also an order of ranking. Conditions of work in the undergraduate college are not as good as in the university department and sometimes they are very bad indeed; the majority of them are controlled either by petty officials or by petty profiteers. The university departments have professors and readers in addition to lecturers whereas the colleges in general have only lecturers. College lecturers do not necessarily have the same scales of pay as university lecturers and, even when they do, their service conditions are generally less favourable. The unionization of teachers has given college lecturers an increasing voice in university affairs and there is growing pressure from the unions for levelling out distinctions of rank within the university.

The goals of university education are many and diverse. Even the most ardent egalitarian will not argue that the pursuit of equality, let

[3] Ibid., p. 77.

alone its attainment, should become the sole concern of the university. At the same time, if this becomes a major concern of the intelligentsia as a whole, it is difficult to see how the universities can remain indifferent to it. Having turned the light of criticism on the social hierarchies outside, the universities cannot screen their own internal arrangements from the same light.

There is hardly any institution in the modern world which provides a more congenial ground than the university for experiments with equality. It brings together individuals from a variety of classes and strata: how successful is it in enabling them to deal with each other 'on individual merit', regardless of social background? To the extent that the university stands between the institutions of home and work, does it do any better than these in dealing with men and women on equal terms, irrespective of sex? Then there is the succession of generations and the question of giving equal consideration to the claims of youth and age; I touch upon this question briefly and incidentally, and only in so far as it concerns the issue of promotion by seniority.

The university has obligations to the wider society outside, and it is often reminded of its obligations by the press, by parliament and by the ministry. Since university education is expensive, and since its expenses are met out of the tax-payer's money, the press and parliament ask for evidence to show that the benefits of university education are widely, if not evenly, distributed throughout society. Any government in a country such as India has to cope with enormous populist pressures, and it is only natural that it should try to pass some of these pressures on to the universities. The universities are generally improvident and can rarely do with what resources they get, hence they are always ready to make concessions to populist pressures if that gets them a little more money.[4]

It is not easy to measure the contribution made by university education to the attainment of equality. For one thing, this contribution may not be direct; for another, it may not be apparent in the short run. We have also to consider the argument that, by diverting scarce resources from primary and secondary education, university education might in fact hinder rather than help the

[4] Edward Shils has made a similar argument about the American university in his Jefferson Lecture, but scarcity and mismanagement make the problem much more acute in the Indian university. See Edward Shils, 'Government and Universities in the United States', *Minerva*, vol. XVII, no. 1, Spring 1979, pp. 129–77.

equalization of opportunities in society as a whole.[5] This is particularly the case in a country like India where large numbers of people
do not get even the benefits of primary education.

Even for countries that can manage to send everybody to school,
there is no clear evidence of the gains to equality from university
education. The rapid expansion of university education does not
guarantee the reduction, not to speak of the elimination, of social
inequality. After noting this expansion in America, a recent study
declares, somewhat indignantly: 'Colleges and universities play a
crucial role in the production of labour power, in the reproduction
of the class structure, and in the perpetuation of the dominant values
of the social order.'[6] Those who hope for the elimination of the class
structure through the expansion of university education will have to
wait for a very long time.

It will be a mistake to think that only radical academics in America
express indignation when they find that their universities are re-
producing the class structure. Such indignation is very widely expressed and perhaps quite widely felt. The Commission on University
Education, set up under the chairmanship of Dr S. Radhakrishnan
shortly after independence, declared: 'Education is a universal right,
not a class privilege.'[7] What the Commission probably had in mind is
that access to the university should not in principle be denied to
anyone, not that in practice everyone who asked for a place in a
university should get one. Nor is it likely that the Commission had
in mind the immediate abolition of the class structure. But this much
ought to be clear, that so long as society has a class structure,
university education will continue to be more or less of a class
privilege.

The concern for equality was carried over into the second major
commission on education set up in independent India, the Education
Commission of 1964–66, under the chairmanship of Dr D. S.
Kothari. The scope of the Kothari Commission was wider than that
of the Radhakrishnan Commission since it covered primary and
secondary in addition to higher education. It not only included the

[5] See Amartya Sen, 'The Crisis in Indian Education' (The Lal Bahadur Shastri
Memorial Lectures, delivered on 10 and 11 March 1970 in New Delhi), cyclo-
styled.

[6] Samuel Bowles and Herbert Gintis, *Schooling in Capitalist America*, Routledge and Kegan Paul, 1976, pp. 201–2.

[7] *The Report of the University Education Commission, 1948–49*, Ministry of
Education, Government of India, 1950, vol. I, p. 50.

attainment of equality among the objectives of education—school education as well as university education—but also assigned a more active role to education as an instrument of social change: 'If this "change on a grand scale" is to be achieved without violent revolution (and even for that it would be necessary) there is one instrument, and one instrument only, that can be used: EDUCATION.'[8]

Actually, both the Commissions produced very sober and judicious Reports, formulating a whole range of goals and objectives for university education, and drawing attention to the practical difficulties of harmonizing them. At the same time, they have served to give shape and substance to the argument that the universities can no longer justify themselves by academic attainments alone, but must orient themselves to a definite social purpose, or even that their academic attainments must be judged in the light of that social purpose.

Edward Shils has argued in his Jefferson Lecture that 'the idea that universities could create social equality' is a new one.[9] In the United States it caught the imagination of the public only after the Second War. This is not to say that in the past people did not recognize that universities could and should be used as means of social ascent by talented individuals lacking the advantages of birth. In fact, special endowments have been made in the universities from the Middle Ages onwards precisely with that end in view. Such a conception of the university does not call for an end to the existing system of stratification but, rather, takes its continued existence for granted. Totally different from it is the conception that the university should play a major part, if not the central part, in transforming a hierarchical society into an egalitarian one, or a class-divided society into a classless one.

It should not be difficult merely to recognize that the pursuit of equality through increased opportunities for individual mobility is different from the creation of equality by abolition of the class structure. What is difficult is to accept all the implications of the distinction without yielding to the temptations of rhetoric. Increasingly, on public occasions such as convocations, academic dignitaries

[8] *Education and National Development: Report of the Education Commission, 1964–66*, NCERT (New Delhi), 1971, p. 8.
[9] Shils, 'Government and Universities in the United States', p. 134.

call upon the universities to take the lead in the creation of full equality, although in private they readily admit that such an objective may not be very realistic, and that the universities should try at least to give more people a better chance.

The Radhakrishnan Commission, which declared that 'education is a universal right, not a class privilege', also pointed out that 'in most countries of the world there is an ordered hierarchy in the universities'.[10] As institutions, the universities have had a very long and a very chequered history, and it is difficult to form a realistic idea of what they may be expected to do without some consideration of their history. The most important part of this history from our point of view lies in the way in which the university has changed from being an institution adapted to a hierarchical social environment to one more in tune with the contemporary spirit of equality.

Indian universities are of relatively recent origin, and the ones that we have today have very little to do with India's 'ancient and medieval centres of learning'.[11] If they have links with the medieval world, then indeed these links go back, through the British universities of the nineteenth century after which they were modelled, to the world of medieval Europe.

The first Indian universities were established in 1857 in the three presidency capitals of Calcutta, Bombay and Madras, and they took the English universities—in particular London as it then was—as their model. There was to be a break with the indigenous intellectual tradition, imprisoned as it was in the immobile world of religion and caste, and an entry into the expanding universe of liberal Western ideas. We must remember that the nineteenth century was a period of great expansion in the building of universities in England where, until the University of Durham was set up in 1832, the two universities of Oxford and Cambridge had between themselves held the field for more than six hundred years.[12] The Indian universities were in their structure very different from Oxford and Cambridge in

---

[10] *Report of the University Education Commission*, pp. 50, 72.

[11] *Education and National Development*, op. cit., p. 7. It cannot be too strongly emphasized that when the first Indian universities were set up in Calcutta, Bombay and Madras in 1857, they were expected to make a clean break with the indigenous intellectual tradition imprisoned in the structure of caste and community.

[12] I exclude the Scottish universities, although we have to remember that in the eighteenth century Edinburgh was a more active centre of learning than Oxford or Cambridge.

either the nineteenth century or earlier, but it would be impossible to exaggerate the significance of these two institutions as ideals of university life and university education in nineteenth-century India, and indeed right until the time of independence.

From the sociological point of view the real achievement of Cambridge and Oxford lies in the success with which they have conducted their passage from the medieval to the modern world.[13] It is not simply that some of the best work in the humanities and the sciences is still conducted there, but also that their roots go directly back into the Middle Ages which are visibly present in them to this day.

The traditions of Oxford and Cambridge reach back into an historical age in which the contemporary concern for equality would appear strange and unfamiliar. Medieval European society was a hierarchical society, and when the first universities were set up—in Bologna, in Paris, in Oxford and in Cambridge—people did not think that the established hierarchy must pass away or that the universities must play a main part in their passing away. On the contrary, the universities not only contributed to the elaboration of the ideas which kept the hierarchy in place, they also reproduced the same hierarchy in the organization of their own internal life. From the twelfth, thirteenth and fourteenth centuries to the fifteenth, sixteenth and seventeenth, the universities of Europe—certainly Oxford and Cambridge—became progressively more hierarchical as they became better endowed and better established.[14]

In the light of what we expect of our universities today, two striking features of these medieval institutions were their close involvement with the church and its hierarchy, and the total exclusion of women from them. Scholars frequently came in order to be trained for the church, and fellows looked to the church for spiritual comfort as well as material advancement: the patronage structure of the university

[13] No doubt this passage appears much more easy today at this distance than it did in eighteenth century England.

[14] The early universities, particularly the 'student-universities' of Italy were in many ways remarkably 'democratic', but these too became rigidly structured with the passage of time. Moreover, 'democracy' in internal arrangements did not mean the absence of 'privileges' in relation to the outside world. In the medieval universities students were no less jealous of their privileges than teachers, and both sought to acquire new privileges while preserving old ones. The standard English work on the subject is Hastings Rashdall, *The Universities of Europe in the Middle Ages*, Oxford University Press, 1936 (new edition), 3 vols.

and its colleges was until quite recent times closely linked with that of the church.[15] The question of equal educational opportunities for women did not arise as the education of women had no place in either Cambridge or Oxford until about a hundred years ago.[16]

Family background had an acknowledged place in the classification of students in Oxford, and the following categories were officially used: *baronis filius* (sons of noblemen), *equitis filius* (sons of knights), *armigeri filius* (sons of esquires), *generosi filius* (sons of gentlemen), *plebei filius* (sons of commoners), and *clerici filius* (sons of clergymen). In keeping with traditional distinctions of status, sons of bishops were listed with sons of noblemen, not of clergymen. Those of inferior status paid smaller fees, but those of superior status were entitled to take first degrees after nine instead of twelve terms of residence. It is noteworthy that these categories were used until as recently as 1891 when the Registrar of Oxford began to record the father's occupation instead of his status.[17] In Cambridge the privilege whereby sons of noblemen were excused from taking examinations (the *ius natalium*) was abolished only in 1884.[18]

The marks of invidious social (as opposed to academic) distinction were visible also in the internal structure of the college. There were the distinctions, first, between master, fellows and students, with their respective privileges. 'Students' themselves were of various kinds. The core consisted of the 'scholars' who, like the fellows, were supported by the foundation: the college provided them with education as well as bed and board. But there were others who had to pay for what the college gave them: these included 'pensioners' who were ordinary fee-paying students in residence, and 'fellow commoners' who paid extra and had the privilege of dining with the fellows. At the bottom were the 'sizars' who, in Cambridge, were granted the

[15] Oxford and Cambridge (and also Paris) were more closely involved in church patronage, particularly after the colleges became established, than the Italian universities which were from the start more secular. But where church patronage was weak, court patronage might be strong, as for example at Padua. See Rashdall, *The Universities of Europe in the Middle Ages*, vol. 2.

[16] In Cambridge two colleges were set up for women in the second half of the nineteenth century. Women were allowed to take the tripos examinations in 1881, but were not allowed immediately to proceed to university degrees. It was only as recently as in 1948 that women were granted full membership of the university.

[17] See Lawrence Stone (ed.), *The University in Society*, Princeton University Press, 1974, vol. I, especially chapters I and III.

[18] Rashdall, *The Universities of Europe in the Middle Ages*, vol. 1, p. 470.

benefits of college life, including college education, in return for menial services rendered to the more privileged members of the college.[19]

Similar distinctions were maintained in the French universities under the *ancien régime*. Philippe Ariès writes: 'An edict of 1626 reveals the existence of similar customs in the colleges of the University of Paris: the colleges separated the boarders from the day-boys, the laymen from the clerics (*domesticos ab externis, a laicis sacerdotis*), but also the sons of good family from the poor students who acted as college servants (*famulos ab ingenuis*).'[20] These distinctions were closely associated with the corporate life of the colleges, and became particularly marked with the dominance of the university by its colleges in Cambridge, Oxford, Paris and elsewhere.

Even older than the colleges and their internal stratification was the preoccupation of the medieval universities with their privileges, liberties and immunities. From what we read about Bologna, Padua and Montpellier, this kind of preoccupation was no less marked in the so-called 'student-universities' than in the 'magisterial universities'.[21] We are struck by the endless petitions from students and masters, jointly and severally, to the authorities—the Pope, the Emperor or the city—for the grant, extension or restoration of legal and quasi-legal privileges of every conceivable kind. Medieval society was one in which people worried little about equality in the abstract and much about privileges in the concrete, and the medieval university fought hard for its privileges and watched over them with a jealous eye.[22]

[19] There is a vast literature on the Cambridge and Oxford colleges to which annalists, historians, biographers, novelists and a host of others have contributed. One gets interesting accounts in the two series of volumes on the Oxford and Cambridge colleges, *College Histories (1895–1911)*, written by fellows of the respective colleges.

[20] Philippe Ariès, *Centuries of Childhood*, Penguin Books, 1979, p. 296.

[21] For the distinction between 'universities of students' and 'universities of masters', and a general discussion of their privileges in the Middle Ages, see Rashdall, *The Universities of Europe in the Middle Ages*, vol. 1.

[22] The charter issued to the University of Vienna by Duke Rudolf IV in 1365 was generous in the immunities and privileges it granted. 'Charges against a master or a scholar, which would be capital in the case of an unprivileged layman, were to be tried, not (as at Paris) by the bishop, but by the chancellor ... A number of special and unprecedented privileges are conferred for the protection of scholars and the benefit of the university. Property confiscated for outrages on scholars was to be divided between the university and the injured party. The

If I have dwelt on the place of privilege and patronage in some of
the most renowned universities in the world, I have not done so in
order to argue that merit did not find any place in them. It would be
capricious to maintain that Cambridge and Oxford devoted all their
attention to social origin and none to individual merit. Their history
in almost every century is too full of illustrious names in every field
of learning to allow such an argument to be taken seriously.

The point I wish to make is simply that an institutional order
based on privilege and patronage might still have within itself considerable room for the recognition, cultivation and promotion of
individual merit. This may sound paradoxical in terms of our modern
conceptions of fairness and justice, but the historical evidence quite
clearly shows the capacity of institutions to accommodate contradictory principles, or principles that appear to be contradictory.
Indeed, it is their capacity to accommodate such principles that gives
to institutions their living quality and ensures their viability by
enabling them to adapt themselves to changing historical conditions.

There is need to emphasize the dynamic tension between the
attention to social distinction and the recognition of individual
merit within the older universities right until the end of the nineteenth century. No one will say that a privileged social background
counts for nothing in Oxford or Cambridge today, but attention to
it has become muted and has had to yield ground to other considerations. Throughout the last hundred years people from an increasingly
varied social background have found their way to these institutions,
occupying positions of distinction in them.[23] The demands at home
and abroad of an expanding capitalist economy played some part in
this in the nineteenth century, and the two World Wars in the
twentieth.

Through all the changes that these older universities have under-

assailant of a scholar lost the benefit of sanctuary. Special protection in travelling
was promised with the usual exemptions from tolls and municipal taxes. If a
scholar was robbed, the duke would compensate the loss. In Vienna itself a
special quarter of the town was granted for the accommodation of students with
a right to demand such houses as they pleased for their residence, the rent to be
fixed by the usual method of arbitration' (Rashdall, *The Universities of Europe in
the Middle Ages*, vol. 2, pp. 237–8).

[23] Jews, Asians or women can now attain the highest academic positions in
Oxford and Cambridge in marked contrast to what prevailed until only a hundred
years ago.

gone since the end of the last century, their institutional basis has remained secure and dependable. Their legitimacy as institutions designed primarily for the pursuit of learning has never been seriously threatened. The Indian universities enjoy nothing like the same kind of legitimacy. The institutional arrangements for even such routine activities as the completion of courses or the conduct of examinations are insecure and undependable. Those who seek to put on them the whole burden of initiating and carrying through a momentous social transformation do not always remember how weak and infirm they are as institutions.

As compared with England till the end of the nineteenth century or even later, the universities in India have been far in advance of society in repudiating traditional social distinctions. In England certain distinctions continued to be maintained, at least in the older universities, long after they had become obsolete or anachronistic in the wider society.[24] There is nothing in the constitution of the modern Indian university which requires the maintenance or even the recognition of the traditional distinctions between castes or between the sexes. These distinctions are nevertheless carried into it from the environment on which it depends for its supply of students and teachers, and it has to devise ways and means of dealing with them. Oxford and Cambridge in the nineteenth century maintained many medieval features in a society in which characteristically modern ways of life were becoming established. In Calcutta, Bombay and Madras, on the other hand, the universities were struggling to emerge as islands of modernity in a society still set largely in its traditional hierarchical mould.

Originating in the nineteenth century, the Indian universities were imbued with the characteristic liberal enthusiasm for opening careers to talent. The liberal concern for the individual, irrespective of race, caste and creed, is the guiding principle of the entire Report of the Radhakrishnan Commission: 'The fundamental right is the right of

[24] 'Only in the universities did the regulation of dress on class lines survive into modern times. Ordered for Cambridge by Burghley in 1578, noblemen continued to wear distinctive dress heavily ornamented with gold lace until the middle of the nineteenth century' (Lawrence Stone, *The Crisis of the Aristocracy 1558–1641*, Clarendon Press, 1965, p. 29).

the individual, not of the community. Every young man must have an equal chance with others to make the most of his abilities.'[25] To the extent that the Indian university seeks to give primacy to the individual, it is and must remain at odds with the structure of traditional Indian society or what survives of it.

I would like to emphasize the lack of harmony between the organizing principle of the university, as seen, for instance, by the Radhakrishnan Commission, and the traditional institutions of village, caste and joint family.[26] While the modern university is different in its orientation from these institutions or even antithetical to them, it cannot be segregated from their influence, precisely because no university in the modern world can be insulated from its social environment. It is this that makes it particularly important for us to realize that the institutional foundations of the Indian University are weak and infirm, whereas the scope and pervasiveness of the traditional institutions are far-reaching, not to say overwhelming. We can no longer believe, as we could to some extent when the country became independent, that time and the mere expansion of higher education would sweep all traditional barriers aside. We now know that this expansion itself can be made to serve the interests of caste and community: I refer not merely to the luxuriant growth of caste-based colleges,[27] but also to the reinforcement of the communal character of an institution such as the Aligarh Muslim University.

If the institutional foundations of the Indian university are weak and infirm, this is at least partly because its span of existence has not been very long: we must never make the mistake of measuring the life-span of institutions by that of individuals. Even though the first three universities were established in 1857—at about the same time as some of the great civic universities in England—they did not for

[25] *Report of the University Education Commission*, vol. I, p. 52. Again, 'Of the end-products of the university, the education of the individual should take priority' (ibid., p. 344).

[26] Compare Nehru on the structure of traditional Indian society: 'This structure was based on three concepts: the autonomous village community, caste and the joint family system. In all these three it is the group that counts: the individual has a secondary place' (Jawaharlal Nehru, *The Discovery of India*, Asia Publishing House, 1961, pp. 247–8).

[27] There is a considerable literature on caste-based educational institutions in the various parts of the country. For an excellent case study, see T. N. Madan and B. G. Halbar, 'Caste and Community in the Private and Public Education of Mysore State' in S. H. Rudolph and L. I. Rudolph (eds.), *Education and Politics in India*, Harvard University Press, 1972, pp. 121–47.

at least the first fifty years of their existence have anything of the corporate character of the older European universities.[28] Throughout the nineteenth century, the first Indian universities confined themselves almost entirely to regulating courses of study and conducting examinations. Since they did no teaching or research, there was hardly any academic staff and only a meagre administrative staff: '... persons eminent in literature and science acted as Boards of Examiners and persons known for their administrative and public services were nominated as the Chancellor, Vice-Chancellor and the Fellows, who together constituted the Body corporate of the University.'[29]

In 1916, under the Vice-Chancellorship of Sir Ashutosh Mukherji, the University of Calcutta took the lead in establishing Postgraduate Departments of its own, and set about appointing University professors and lecturers. Bombay and Madras followed after, although at least until the time of independence Calcutta continued to enjoy pre-eminence in research, particularly scientific research. At the same time, examining remained a major concern, and in Calcutta it began to paralyse administrative work and, after that, academic work within a decade or two of independence. Calcutta, Bombay and Madras set precedents for the universities in pre-independence India by having first an establishment for dealing with examinations and then organizing teaching and research: the University of Delhi, which was established in 1922, appointed its first Professor only in 1942.

By the time the country became independent nearly a hundred years after the first universities were set up, the idea at least had taken root that a university must have a corporate character from the very start, that it must concern itself with teaching and research and not just examining. This clearly is the idea of the new university we find expressed in the Report of the Radhakrishnan Commission, and it is embodied in the new central universities set up since independence. An outstanding example is the Jawaharlal Nehru University, established in 1968, which from the start has had not only students, but

[28] Lord Curzon had observed: 'How different is India! Here the university has no corporate existence in the same (i.e., as Oxford or Cambridge) sense of the term: it is not a collection of buildings, it is scarcely even a site. It is a body that controls courses of study and sets examination papers to pupils of affiliated colleges'. Quoted in *Education and National Development*, p. 498.

[29] Champa Tickoo, *Indian Universities*, Orient Longman, 1980, p. 13.

10

also professors, readers and lecturers; libraries and laboratories; classrooms and hostels; and, above all, a campus of its own with an energetic campus life. It has deliberately restricted the number of students in order to maintain a student–teacher ratio consistent with a healthy corporate life. Unlike the run-of-the-mill university in pre-independence India, which had little room for research, the Jawaharlal Nehru University has concentrated much effort on research; it has perhaps gone to the other extreme by keeping more or less clear of involvement in undergraduate teaching and examining.

In nineteenth-century India the focus of corporate academic life— a life of interaction between students and teachers—was not the university but the college. Colleges were already in existence when, in 1857, the first three universities were established. Hindu College (which later became Presidency College) was established in Calcutta in 1817; Elphinstone College in Bombay in 1834; and Presidency College in Madras in 1840. Throughout the nineteenth century it was to colleges such as these that students came for higher education. The universities were there to maintain uniformity of standards by regulating courses of study and conducting examinations. The establishment of the universities also gave an enormous boost to the establishment of new colleges all over the country.

One cannot emphasize too strongly the part played by these nineteenth-century colleges in the creation of a new social class and a new kind of sensibility. It was here that the 'modernization' of India began, and it was also here that India's 'dependency' on the cultural resources of the West was sealed. These colleges provided not only a new system of knowledge to which many turned with enthusiasm, but also a privileged setting for a new kind of sociality promising inexhaustible possibilities.

The best of the nineteenth-century colleges were established either by the government, for example, Presidency, Calcutta and Elphinstone, Bombay; or by missionaries, for example, St. Xavier's, Calcutta and St. Stephen's, Delhi. In both cases the teachers were often Englishmen or other Europeans. The colleges were small places where close interaction was not only practised but also encouraged. Edward Shils has suggested that, being under the spell of Oxbridge, they concentrated almost exclusively on teaching, and failed to develop a tradition of research.[30] With the establishment of Uni-

[30] See Edward Shils, *The Intellectual Between Tradition and Modernity*, Mouton, 1961.

versity Departments after 1916, and the growing accent on research in them after independence, even the best colleges began to lose the pre-eminence that they had enjoyed for a hundred years.

Today it is accepted by all that the university ought to have a corporate character, that it cannot really flourish in the absence of a 'university community': one no longer asks whether to have a university community or not, one wonders how much of it can be held together. The university campus is a feature of all central universities—which are on the whole the best endowed—although the new ones, like the University of Hyderabad, are still in the stage of construction and the old ones, like the University of Delhi, are already overcrowded. A distinctive feature of the Indian university, at least in the phase during which it has a proper campus, is that it provides, or is expected to provide, housing for staff as well as hostels for students.

The college or the university provides a privileged setting for experiments with a new pattern of relations among persons: this is no less true of Jawaharlal Nehru University in the 1980s than it was of Hindu College in the 1820s. If there is any setting in India in which social relations among persons are relatively unconstrained by tradition, it is neither the office nor the factory, nor even the political party, but the university campus. Nor is this true only of the advanced or liberated campus in the metropolitan city; for life in even the most remote campus in a backward state has a different quality from the general pattern of life in its hinterland. Nothing could be more crass than the belief that young men and women in India come to the universities with the sole object of getting degrees. Young men —and especially young women—also come in order to experience a kind of life which they have never experienced in the home or the neighbourhood and which they fear they may never experience again.

It is well known that colleges and universities in India are in turmoil. The demographic and economic factors behind this turmoil are also well known. The universities are overcrowded, their hostels are inadequate, their libraries and laboratories are ill-equipped, and there is a general lack of facilities in them. Moreover, university education is no longer a guarantee of employment, and the number of unemployed B.A.s, M.A.s and Ph.D.s rises every year. But these material causes do not account for the whole phenomenon since the best-endowed universities, such as the Jawaharlal Nehru University, are no more free from turmoil than the worst-endowed. Beyond the demographic and economic factors there lie social causes: the social world of the university is in fundamental opposition to the social world outside.

The Indian universities and colleges, being modern rather than medieval foundations, never nourished the kinds of invidious distinctions which the European universities had to contend with when they began to modernize themselves in the nineteenth century. They did not grade their students as 'fellow commoners', 'commoners' and 'sizars' in the way in which the colleges in Cambridge and Oxford did for centuries; they did not have different conditions for admission to their degrees for sons of noblemen and sons of commoners as did these universities; and the segregation of women never became an established tradition *within* the university, no matter how strong such a tradition might have been *outside* it. If the historical roots of these universities do not go very deep, this also means that they did not have too many hierarchical traditions to outgrow.

The colleges throughout the nineteenth century, and, when they became established, the universities until the time of independence, accommodated only small numbers of individuals and mainly from the upper strata of society. There might have been attempts from the start to mix the castes and communities promiscuously together within the institution, but that was very different from having them equally, or even equitably represented. These were privileged settings in which people coming mainly, though by no means wholly, from privileged homes sought to establish new norms of social interaction. It is difficult to see what success they could have achieved outside of such small and privileged settings.

But they did achieve some success, and it would be wrong to denigrate or ignore the achievements of the colleges and universities in their early phase of growth. It is true that when we go through the names of the distinguished graduates of Calcutta University, we are struck by the preponderance of names from the three upper castes of Brahmin, Baidya and Kayastha. But from the very early days of Hindu College, the group that formed itself around Derozio had set about ignoring the distinctions of caste, and in the twentieth century Calcutta University not only accommodated but also honoured such men as Brajendranath Seal and Meghnad Saha who came from traditionally disprivileged castes.

With the increase in the number of universities and the growth in their population, the social composition of the university is now more mixed than it used to be. More people now come to the university than before and they come from a wider range of castes, including castes from the middle and the bottom of the traditional hierarchy. Even so, the various castes are not equally represented, or represented in proportion to their strength in the population as a whole. If we go by caste, there clearly is rather better representation than before; if we go by class, in the sense of family income or occupation, the picture is far less clear. This kind of change, particularly since independence, has come about partly through academic competition and partly through political pressure. But the very urge to have a more equitable representation of all the major castes in the university has given a different turn to the initial experiment to create a new pattern of relations within the university community without consideration for caste.

Ironically, it is in the 'élite' institutions, where social and academic privilege is most in evidence, that considerations of caste play the least part in interpersonal relations within the university community. The poorly-endowed provincial universities, which depend almost wholly on their immediate environment for the intake of both students and staff, are more manifestly in the grip of caste and other traditional distinctions. If the role of caste is not evident in the relations between students and teachers in the classrooms, it is certainly evident in the relations among students in the hostels. But even here there is a change: the inequalities of caste have again become manifest not so much because everyone accepts them, as in the past, as because so many are now trying to overthrow them.

There is one area of relation within the university community where change is most marked in the more privileged institutions, although it is evident everywhere: this is the relation between men and women. Women began to make a place for themselves in the universities almost as soon as they came into being in India, unlike in the West where the universities kept women out for centuries during which time they acquired markedly male traditions. The University of Calcutta, set up in 1857, allowed women to take the B.A. examination in 1878 and the first women graduates took their degrees in 1883; the University of Bombay followed shortly after. Colleges for women began to come up in the nineteenth century, and when the postgraduate departments came up, women found their way in there as well.

University and college education for women was a highly restricted affair in the nineteenth century and it remained restricted until the middle of the twentieth. Even today there is no question of absolute equality between men and women in any numerical sense, but the changes in both quantitative and qualitative terms are worth noting. The number of women enrolled as students in colleges and universities rose from six in 1881–2 to 256 in 1901–2, and stood at 23,207 in 1946–7 on the eve of independence.[31] Since then the rise in student enrolment has been very rapid: from 43,126 in 1950–1 to 170,455 in 1960–1 to 655,822 in 1970–1; in relative terms there were 10.9 women for every 100 men in 1950–1, 16.2 in 1960–1 and 21.9 in 1970–1.[32] The number and proportion of women teachers in colleges and universities have also gone up: from 1,815 (8.5 per cent of the total) in 1950–1 to 6,923 (12.5 per cent) in 1960–1 to 19,390 (15.0 per cent) in 1970–1.[33]

It is not necessary to go wholly or even mainly by numbers. Women have by now competed successfully for the best places in university examinations and the highest positions in faculty appointments, not in every university or in every faculty, but in a sufficient number of cases for them to be able to feel secure about their academic achievements within the university. The success of women is particularly visible in the better, metropolitan universities, whether we take the Universities of Calcutta and Bombay among the older ones or Delhi University and Jawaharlal Nehru University among the newer. All of this has been accompanied by a marked change in the social participation of women in the universities, whether as students or as teachers. For women, even more than for men, the university is not only a place of work, it is also a place of recreation, and, for some of them, perhaps the only place of recreation.[34] There is more equality between men and women in both performance and participation in the university than anywhere outside. But we must see this transformation for what it is: it is overwhelmingly, if not entirely, a middle-class, or, if the phrase be preferred, a bourgeois phenomenon.

[31] Government of India, *Towards Equality: Report of the Committee on the Status of Women in India*, Department of Social Welfare (Government of India), 1974, p. 238.   [32] Ibid., p. 241.   [33] Ibid., p. 260.

[34] Karuna Ahmad, 'They accept college education as something which has to be undertaken and which serves to absolve them of all responsibilities at home. To most of them it is an extension of their adolescence and keeps them away from the burden of housekeeping.' 'Social Background of Women Undergraduates of Delhi University', unpublished Ph.D. thesis, University of Delhi, 1968, p. 108.

The Scheduled Castes (Harijans) and the Scheduled Tribes (Adivasis) constitute a tiny section of the middle class, unlike women who make up half of it. Together these two groups of communities comprise over twenty per cent of the total population of the country. They have for centuries been socially and economically disadvantaged and, although their disabilities have been removed by law, they continue to suffer from a number of disadvantages in fact. The progress of education, particularly higher education, has been slow among them, despite attempts by the government to hasten it through freeships and scholarships.[35] Social prejudice has to some extent obstructed the academic achievements of the Harijans and Adivasis, but a more serious obstacle today is the abject poverty of the vast majority of them to whom even the benefit of literacy comes very slowly.

The number of lecturers belonging to the Scheduled Castes and Scheduled Tribes is small, and the number of readers and professors much smaller: 46 readers out of a total of nearly 7,000 and 20 professors out of a total of over 3,000.[36] Once again, the question is not simply of numbers. Harijans and Adivasis have not become a visible or significant academic presence on the campus, whether among students or among teachers.[37] This is particularly true of the more esteemed metropolitan universities such as those of Calcutta, Bombay and Delhi.

The way in which the gap between men and women has been narrowed in the university stands in marked contrast to the continuing gap between the upper castes and the lower, or between the middle class and other social classes. It tells us a great deal about how far the universities can go in the creation of equality, but it also tells us something about the ways in which discrimination operates in the larger society. There is no doubt about the discrimination that existed

[35] For the impact of higher education on the Harijans see Suma Chitnis, 'Education for Equality: Case of Scheduled Castes in Higher Education', *Economic and Political Weekly*, vol. 7, Nos. 31–33 (Special Number), August 1972, pp. 1675–81.

[36] University Grants Commission, *Report for the Year 1978–79*, New Delhi, n.d., pp. 210–14. The U.G.C. *Report* for 1979–80 does not give figures for professors and readers, but shows a figure of 287 lecturers belonging to the Scheduled Castes and Scheduled Tribes out of a total of 16,444 lecturers, i.e. 1.75 per cent of the total.

[37] There have, however, been occasions when political conditions have made them highly visible as, for instance, at Marathwada University during the agitation over renaming the University after the great Harijan leader, Dr B. R. Ambedkar.

and continues to exist between men and women within the family, but the discrimination that operates within the family is different not just in degree but in kind from the one that operates between castes and between classes. To be sure, middle class parents discriminate between their sons and their daughters, but they do not discriminate between them in at all the same way in which they discriminate between their own children and the children of others.

I have tried to argue that the Indian universities have made some progress in the pursuit of equality in at least some directions. But they have not all moved forward to the same extent in every direction, and some appear, at least from certain points of view, to be moving backwards. Paradoxically, it is in the most 'privileged', or 'élitist' or 'exclusive' institutions that the relations among castes or between the sexes are least marked by the kind of invidious distinctions that have been traditionally their most remarkable feature.

If the universities can supersede the invidious distinctions upheld by tradition only by remaining as privileged enclaves in the larger society, we must ask how far they can be expected to go in their efforts to create social equality. Clearly, they have other aims and responsibilities, including the creation of new knowledge and the promotion of individual talent and ability. The university has to ensure, if it is to function as a place of learning, that those whom it admits to its membership or to its degrees have the capacity to measure up to its academic demands. As the Radhakrishnan Commission put it, tersely, 'Intellectual work is not for all, it is only for the intellectually competent.'[38]

Some might feel uneasy about having to reconcile the dictum that 'intellectual work is not for all' with the sentiment that 'education is a universal right'. To be sure, the two may easily be reconciled in principle by requiring, firstly, that certain forms of discrimination be rigorously excluded from the university, and, secondly, that certain other forms of discrimination be applied equally rigorously. But there are enormous practical difficulties in ensuring that these two seemingly simple requirements be simultaneously met, and it is impossible to escape the suspicion that the wrong kind of discrimination is being made under cover of the right one. Such suspicion is present in all universities in the modern world, but it is endemic in India

[38] *Report of the University Education Commission*, p. 98.

where traditional distinctions are all-pervasive outside the university, while within it academic standards are weak and unreliable.

How does a university make its academic standards firm and reliable, and how does it create confidence among people in its academic standards? There can be no general answers to such questions, and we can go only by historical examples. The European universities did not acquire their acknowledged place in public life in a day or even a century. Oxford and Cambridge had passed through many vicissitudes before successfully evolving their own criteria of discrimination as a result of centuries of trial and error.[39] Our own universities have had little time to grow into institutions with their own criteria of discrimination, accepted within and acknowledged outside. They had hardly settled down to an academic existence before being caught in the toils of nationalist politics, radical politics, and, above all, populist politics.

To discriminate consistently according to academic criteria alone is a difficult undertaking, and there are many diversions along its exacting course. Success in such an undertaking calls for a capacity for independent judgement and a respect for independent judgement that come only from long experience. It is a part of the routine of every university to exercise such academic judgement in the admission of students, the award of scholarships and fellowships, the appointment and promotion of faculty members, and so on. No university can ensure fully against errors of judgement in any of these matters; but, where many are called but few are chosen, as in the Indian universities, it takes little to convince people that academic judgement is generally—or even necessarily—vitiated by social or political prejudice.

It will be difficult to pretend that there is in India very much confidence in the university's capacity to exercise academic judgement without fear or favour. The lack of confidence is not only widespread outside the university, it is conspicuous inside it as well. A clear indication of this is the increasing amount of litigation in which the universities have become involved over appointments, over ad-

[39] Rashdall tells us of a long phase in the history of Oxford during which 'the university teaching practically disappeared, and the university degree system, having no organic relation to the real studies of the college, degenerated into a farce' (Rashdall, *The Universities of Europe in the Middle Ages*, vol. 2, p. 321). See also Sheldon Rothblatt, 'The Student Sub-culture and Examination System in Early 19th Century Oxbridge', in Stone (ed.), *The University in Society*, vol. 1, pp. 247–303.

missions and over examinations. There are universities that have acquired a certain notoriety by making appointments on considerations other than those of merit; the pendulum has now swung to the other extreme, and the 'stay order' from the High Court against appointments has become almost a routine in some of them.

It will be absurd to argue that scholastic ability and academic attainment count for nothing in university appointments and admissions, even if we concede that other considerations count for something in them. Although such comparisons may not reveal very much, it will be a fair guess that at least in the better Indian universities academic considerations still count for rather more in admissions and appointments than they did in, let us say, eighteenth-century Oxford. But perhaps what matters more than the selection procedures actually used is the confidence of people in the fairness of these procedures, and there is little doubt that this confidence has declined during the last thirty years. It is this erosion of confidence that puts people in the mood to argue—not always seriously, but with a certain insistence—that since the universities have failed in their academic responsibilities, they ought to justify themselves by contributing more directly to social reform if not to social revolution.

Even where academic criteria are not strictly adhered to in appointments and admissions, it does not follow that this is because discrimination is being practised, consciously or unconsciously, in accordance with traditional principles of exclusion. Firstly, academic criteria themselves are not always or even generally unambiguous. Secondly, their true nature and significance are not always understood by those who have the responsibility to apply them. Thirdly, those who seek to manipulate the system use quite complicated calculations, leading to gradations that differ, and sometimes differ quite widely, from the gradations of the traditional order. Even those who might like to uphold the invidious distinctions of the past cannot any longer do so openly within the university, but have to act under the cover of upholding academic ability and academic efficiency.

Far from eliminating all forms of inequality, the modern university creates new inequalities, but by a process of competition in which 'pure merit' is believed to count as against race, caste or sex, or what is loosely described as 'social background'. It is not as if there are no critics of the new inequality of merit established by the university, particularly through its examination system.[40] Two kinds

[40] A great deal has been written on the subject since Michael Young published *The Rise of the Meritocracy*, Thames and Hudson, 1958.

of criticism are commonly made against it. The first is that the excesses of untempered competition are of high cost to the individual and to society as a whole as seen from the human point of view.[41] The second criticism is that the inequalities established by competition do not tell us much about merit in any fundamental sense, but only about performance of a particular kind.[42]

Ideally, it might appear possible to separate out the contribution to scholastic achievement or academic success of 'pure merit' from that of 'social background'. In practice it is difficult, if not impossible, to do this. I am not now talking only about the difficulty of separating out the contributions of 'heredity' and of 'environment' to intelligence,[43] because academic appointments and admissions are not made on the basis of 'generalized intelligence' and are not claimed to be made on that basis. The university claims merely that it disregards social background, selecting persons according to a particular kind of ability, wherever such ability might be found.

Now, it is well known that ability of the kind valued by the university is not found evenly distributed among the strata, and between men and women. This being the case, one would expect men from the upper strata to be represented in excess of their proportion in the population, without the university consciously discriminating against either women or the lower strata in its admissions and appointments. In other words, the university tends to reproduce, at least to some extent, the existing inequalities in society. But it must be realized that when this happens, the responsbility for it does not rest only with the university; at least in the case of the disparities between men and women, it rests much more with the family.

Perhaps one might say that people can be taken on by the university only where they are left off by the family and the school. The university does not have access to individuals in their natural condi-

---

[41] As a well-known English academic, the Provost of King's College, wrote: 'The more "successful" your education, the more likely you are to feel alone, because the process of segregation has been more complete. Just a few of you are academics like myself. 11+, O Level, A Level, College Entrance, Degree Class, Ph.D. . . . at every stage you proved how much cleverer you are than all those other fellows, until in the end you stand quite alone and afraid' (Edmund Leach, *A Runaway World?*, British Broadcasting Corporation, 1968, p. 73).

[42] See my Auguste Comte Memorial Lecture, 1979, *The Idea of Natural Inequality*, republished in this volume, pp. 7–32.

[43] There is a vast literature on the subject to which biologists, psychologists, sociologists and others have contributed. Two works representing opposite points of view are, H. J. Eysenck, *The Inequality of Man*, Fontana, 1975, and L. J. Kamin, *The Science and Politics of IQ*, Lawrence Erlbaum Associates, 1974.

tion. If the schools prepare children from the different strata un-equally for university education, the university might cancel out some of these inequalities, but not all of them. If the family does not prepare its sons and its daughters with the same care for school education, the school can—if it has the will—make good the dis-parity to some extent but not to the full extent.

The university can to some extent correct the disparities due to social background with which its population is already encumbered at the time of entry into it. It can do this to some extent because the family, the school and the other institutions of society might stifle but cannot destroy the capacity for intellectual growth among indi-viduals against whom they discriminate on social grounds, i.e. on the ground that they are women or of a lower caste or an inferior race. In regard to women this is proved by the many examples of great academic success, particularly in the better Indian universities during the last two or three decades.[44] It is true, nonetheless, that the indi-vidual must have more than average intellectual ability in order to attain average academic success if he or she has also to overcome the disadvantages of social background.

The Indian university is not always able to provide the kind of congenial setting that makes it easy for talented individuals to over-come the disadvantages of social background. It is not always possessed of a clear judgement of the issues involved, and, even when it has the judgement, it might lack the will to act in accordance with it. Its judgement is clouded and its will sapped by too many pressures from within and outside. It is difficult for the university to maintain clarity of judgement and firmness of will in the handling of social problems once it begins to lose confidence in its academic standards. The feeling that it can and must create social equality here and now is easily replaced by the mood that it can do nothing to reduce the disparities between individuals that they owe to their social back-ground unless the government or some other political agency in-tervenes and imposes a radical solution from outside.

We cannot, in the modern world, expect the university to remain fully insulated from external political pressures. The universities are

_____

[44] One can argue that this has been due primarily to changes in attitudes to-wards boys and girls within the middle class family, particularly among pro-fessional people.

in fact more exposed to the outside world today than they have ever been before, and we need not take very seriously those academic enthusiasts who seek the intervention of their chosen party—either the ruling party or an opposition party—in order to secure full autonomy for their university. At the same time, we cannot remain heedless of the cost to the academic life of the university every time we invite the intervention of government in its affairs. There are those in the university who are always ready to do a little more for the promotion of social justice, fearing that they can do very little to redeem its academic fortunes. And there are those in the government who are quite happy to pass on to the university as many of their own social and political responsibilities as they can safely discard.

Thirty-three years after independence Indians with a social conscience have begun to feel that the universities have made little if any tangible contribution to the spread of equality in their society. They have begun to wonder what became of all the Plans that were made for directing education to a new social purpose, and to ask where all the money went that was poured in for the building of new universities and the expansion of old ones. Perhaps the universities might have done a little more than they actually did; certainly, they have done much less than they were expected to do.

In a society which is divided into innumerable tribes, clans, castes, sects and denominations in addition to various linguistic, religious and other minorities, and where collective identities are very marked, people find it natural to ask whether the proportion of university graduates (or of college lecturers) in their community is equal to, greater than or less than their proportion in some other community or in society as a whole. In fact, this is one of the characteristic forms, if not the most characteristic form, in which the problem of equality is coming to be posed in contemporary India. And a whole new language of discourse—involving phrases such as 'backwards' and 'forwards', 'minorities' and 'majorities', 'quotas' and 'reservations'[45] —has begun to animate the debate on equality and social justice.

It will be a mistake to think that the frame of mind described above is unknown outside India. It is fairly common in other Asian countries and seems to be rapidly gaining ground in at least the

---

[45] It has now become fairly common in certain parts of India to say of a certain individual that 'he is a Backward', or of a certain set of individuals that 'they are Forwards'.

universities in the United States, despite the pronounced individualism characteristic of that society. Those responsible for making
appointments in the American universities have now to pay attention
to achieving and maintaining some kind of balance between the
claims of men and women and of the various ethnic groups. Not to
have any women, Blacks or Hispanics on the faculty is to expose it to
the charge of practising discrimination against them, for it is undoubtedly the case that they are grossly under-represented in the
American university. Again, in America as in India, the government
is deeply involved in this process, and Edward Shils has charged it
with wishing 'to displace intellectual criteria and to diminish their
importance in order to elevate ethnic and sexual criteria' in the
selection process.[46]

I consider the American example to be of very great significance
because it shows that even in a society which places the highest value
on individualism, the 'quota principle' can make some room for
itself. But there are also profound differences between India and
America. American society lacks the multiplicity of castes and communities characteristic of India, hence there the main emphasis is
likely to be on quotas for women, whereas in India the special claims
of castes and communities are likely to receive far greater public
attention. Caste quotas are very much in harmony with the character
of Indian politics, which is not to say that ethnic quotas are unknown
in American politics. However, the most important difference is that
academic life in America, unlike in India, stands on firm institutional
foundations; hence the American university has better resources than
the Indian to contain social demands that are not necessarily consistent with academic requirements.

In India the principle of caste quotas in public appointments has
been officially accepted for a long time. The British shaped it into an
instrument of policy from a characteristic combination of moral and
tactical considerations: they felt some genuine concern for the advancement of socially-disprivileged persons, but they also found it
convenient to keep the natives divided. The quota principle did not
lose ground after independence, as some had hoped it might, but
became more firmly entrenched. It is true that university appointments are not made directly by the government, but they are widely
viewed as being analogous to government appointments. A government committed to democracy and development is expected to have

[46] Shils, 'Government and Universities in the United States', p. 144.

a socially-relevant employment policy, and, where university education has grown largely on the initiative of government, as in India,
people naturally expect the universities to make their appointments
within the framework of that policy.

It cannot be too strongly emphasized that in India for many, perhaps most, people university employment is a kind of government
service. University and college teachers, in their turn, see themselves
as being more like civil servants than like doctors, lawyers or writers.
It is true that the bureaucratization of the academic profession has
taken place to some extent everywhere, but in India it was there from
the very start. The first universities were set up by the government,
but, before that, there were the government colleges like Presidency
and Elphinstone where professors were and still are appointed on
terms and conditions modelled on the civil service. The Indian
Educational Service was in fact a branch of the civil service and its
members, who occupied senior staff positions in the better government colleges, enjoyed in their time (1864–1924) as much prestige as
the professors in the best Indian universities.[47]

It will be impossible to understand the pressures on the universities
to promote equality by becoming more representative without some
understanding of the political compulsions of job reservation. Today
job reservation enjoys the support of all political parties, although
some might support it mainly out of prudence. The strong advocates
of job reservation appeal to the Constitution, but the constitutional
position is neither clear nor specific. Art. 335 of the Constitution
merely says that the 'claims of the members of the Scheduled Castes
and the Scheduled Tribes shall be taken into consideration . . . in the
making of appointments to services and posts in connection with the
affairs of the Union or of a State'. This is a weak recommendation in
comparison with the clear provisions in Arts. 330 and 332 regarding the proportions of seats in Parliament and the Assemblies to
be actually reserved for the Scheduled Castes and the Scheduled
Tribes.

Job reservation is in fact practised much more systematically and
extensively than is strictly required by the letter of Art. 335 or the
more capacious Art. 46 which directs the State to 'promote with
special care the educational and economic interests of the weaker

---

[47] For a brief account of the service, see Irene A. Gilbert, 'The Organization of
the Academic Profession in India: The Indian Educational Service, 1864–1924'
in Rudolph and Rudolph (eds.), *Education and Politics in India*, pp. 319–41.

sections of the people'. There are specific quotas for the Scheduled Castes and the Scheduled Tribes for appointments as well as promotions to posts in the various branches of the government. But more important than that, there are in many states quotas for a whole range of castes and communities over and above the Scheduled Castes and Scheduled Tribes on the ground that they also constitute 'backward classes' or 'weaker sections' of society. Sometimes these weaker sections are able to use very strong political pressures to have their weakness officially acknowledged. Till the sixties the Supreme Court sought to restrict the use of caste quotas, but in recent years it appears to be taking a more tolerant view, admitting reservations even beyond fifty per cent of the positions available.[48]

It is difficult to determine the correct moral position on a question of this kind, or even to decide whether there has to be only one correct position. The principle of equal opportunity cannot be tested in a vacuum, it has to be judged by its fruits. It will be unreasonable to complain when equality of opportunity leads to inequality of result, for that is a necessary consequence of academic competition. But there will be reason for misgiving when the inequalities that result from academic competition reproduce identically the same pattern of inequalities that prevailed in the traditional order. This misgiving will be reinforced when there is independent evidence of social prejudice in the university against traditionally-disprivileged strata. It will then be up to the university to take note of such evidence, to keep a watchful eye on social prejudice, and to construct selection procedures with built-in correctives against it. It is true that the line between social prejudice and academic discrimination is a thin one, but the university must bear the responsibility of drawing it, for no other agency can draw it.

Those outside the university must realize that even if the university succeeds in eliminating all social prejudice from its selection procedures, the inequalities generated by academic competition will at best differ somewhat, but not a great deal, from the inequalities of the traditional order. Men and women students, students from professional and peasant families, Brahmin and Harijan students are very differently equipped intellectually by the time they seek admission to the university at the age of nineteen or twenty. It would be

---

[48] The position seems to be by no means settled, but compare, for instance, M. R. Balaji *vs.* State of Mysore (*A.I.R. 1963 S.C.* 649) with State of Kerala *vs.* N. M. Thomas (*A.I.R. 1976 S.C.* 490).

foolish and irresponsible to expect the university to wipe all these differences away by the wave of a magic wand. Anyone who has taught in a university knows how little he can do to alter the mental habits of students who have passed their teens, and how hard it is at that age to raise the ill-equipped student to even the level of the average. So if students leave the university in roughly the same order of rank in which they enter it, that is not necessarily because those who start at the bottom are prevented from moving up in the order by the active operation of social prejudice within the university.

Thus we must clearly distinguish between two things: on the one hand, the elimination of all forms of social prejudice against the traditionally-disprivileged sections of the population; and, on the other, the creation of a faculty or a student body in which all sections of society will be represented in proportion to their strength in the population. It cannot be too strongly emphasized that the second objective cannot be automatically realized by simply eliminating prejudice within the university, while leaving untouched the other institutions of society, e.g. its domestic and economic institutions. No doubt, a representative character may be artificially imposed on the university from outside by a comprehensive system of quotas. But that is more likely to prevent than to promote the equal parti- cipation of all individual members of the university in its corporate life.

Every time a candidate of superior academic merit is passed over to make place for one who is less than his academic equal, some damage is done to the foundations on which the university stands. It is not clear that the damage becomes smaller when justification for such action is sought in the need for creating parity between castes. One may doubt whether it is at all possible in this day and age to establish parity between castes, and whether it is worth trying to pursue such an elusive objective at the cost of the individual.

The University Education Commission of 1948–49 had warned against the consequences of the 'rationing of seats' among castes and communities. Its argument against such rationing was that 'It would tend to increase the stratification of our society. To insist on quotas for communities would be to assume that the nation is composed of separate and self-sufficient groups, which is a negation of our national ideal and democratic principle. Discrimination practices generate tensions and the spiritual damage caused by them is not measurable. Education should not be used for creating or deepening the very

11

inequalities which it is designed to prevent'.[49] In other words, the university cannot pay its debt to society by sacrificing individual merit on the plea of promoting parity between castes; the attempt to promote such parity will lead not to the weakening of caste but to its strengthening.

If the university is to play any part in freeing society from the grip of traditional distinctions, it must promote the individual as against caste and community. To be sure, it must attend to special needs where such needs exist, just as it must encourage and reward outstanding merit wherever such merit is found. But these special needs must be seen as the needs of individuals, just as outstanding merit is always recognized as individual merit. The university as we know it today is equipped to attend to the special needs only of individuals, and not of castes and communities. If it tries to attend to the needs of castes and communities, it cannot remain what it is. It cannot distribute its rewards—whether examination grades, or scholarships or faculty appointments—on the basis of quotas determined by political bargains. Above all, universities should not allow themselves to become hunting grounds for leaders of castes and communities negotiating for shares in their rewards for their own constituents, irrespective of merit. They will contribute little, if anything, to the attainment of equality in that way, and they will certainly undermine their own institutional foundations in the process.

In a country with a vast population of illiterates, university graduates are a privileged category by the very fact of having been through a university. But this is not necessarily how it appears to them. A university degree is a necessity for the better kind of employment, but it is no longer a guarantee of any kind of employment. The large increase since independence in the number of universities has been accompanied by a corresponding increase in the number of unemployed graduates. Having to bear the responsibility for the overproduction of graduates, the universities are particularly sensitive to pressures for the creation of additional employment for them. The most direct way of responding to these pressures is of course to ask for the creation of more employment within the academic system by adding to the posts in the existing universities and colleges, and by establishing new colleges and new universities.

There is a close and acknowledged link between the expansion of

[49] *Report of the University Education Commission*, p. 52.

university education and the problem of employment. It would be futile to pretend in a country like India that the university needs to attend only to 'academic' problems, leaving other institutions to deal with 'social' problems. The university cannot insulate itself from social problems, and the most pressing among these is the problem of employment: fair employment, just employment, equitable employment, and, above all, more employment. In India the successful academic must be able to find or create jobs for at least some of his students; to pretend to judge him solely by his qualities as a scholar or a teacher would be disingenuous.

It is impossible to create or find jobs in the university without recourse to government. Indian universities are in theory autonomous institutions, governed by their own Acts, Statutes and Ordinances. In practice, however, their dependence for funds on government requires them to bring their rules of appointment and promotion into alignment with government policy on employment. The manœuvres through which this alignment is brought about are varied and complex, but some sacrifice has always to be made of academic criteria to what the government of the day considers to be the criteria of social justice. Two conspicuous examples of this are appointment according to community and promotion according to seniority, both of which are advocated as measures of justice and equity without consideration for the specific needs and objectives of universities as institutions.

From time to time news items appear in the press about measures being contemplated by government to remedy the inadequate representation of socially backward communities on university and college faculties. According to a newspaper report, 'A statement circulated among the members of a parliamentary committee shows that there is no lecturer belonging to Scheduled Castes or Tribes in Aligarh, Hyderabad and Jawaharlal Nehru Universities while there are three each in Banaras and Delhi universities and one in Viswabharati.'[50] There were indications of threats by or on behalf of the University Grants Commission to stop the flow of funds to these universities if they failed to remedy this lack of representation.

Various parties are involved in these pressures to ensure equity between castes and communities within the university. Apart from the legislatures and the ministries of the union and state governments, there are the University Grants Commission and the Commissioner

[50] *The Times of India*, New Delhi, 11 April 1981.

for Scheduled Castes and Scheduled Tribes. The office of the Commissioner is an important one, created under the Constitution of India to watch over the interests of the Scheduled Castes and Scheduled Tribes. In recent years successive Commissioners have increasingly argued for the reservation of jobs in virtually every area of public life. The models in all such cases are the services under the union and state governments where strict and elaborate procedures have been laid down for the reservation of posts for various castes and communities.

The Commissioner for Scheduled Castes and Scheduled Tribes has for over a decade recommended the reservation of lectureships in universities for the Scheduled Castes and Scheduled Tribes. Finding the response of the universities to be less than satisfactory, the Commissioner 'suggested that a directive should be issued to all the Universities making it obligatory on their part to introduce this reservation. The University Grants Commission has, however, expressed its inability to issue such a directive as U.G.C. Act does not empower it to do so. The Ministry of Education and the University Grants Commission have, therefore, been advised by the Commissioner to ensure that the Act is suitably amended so as to enable the University Grants Commission to issue a directive to all the Universities for implementation of the safeguards in service matters.'[51] The amendment of the Act, it hardly needs to be said, will have far-reaching consequences for the central universities which have so far successfully resisted pressures from such quarters to alter the conditions of academic appointments.

The state universities have been, on the whole, more accommodating in these matters. Job reservation in general has been a major issue of public policy in the southern states, particularly Karnataka, Kerala and Tamilnadu, to a larger extent than in north India. Parties with very different political complexions have been in office in these states, yet they have all accepted job reservation on a very wide scale. Firstly, a very large number of communities in addition to the Scheduled Castes and Scheduled Tribes have been granted concessions in the matter of employment; secondly, such concessions have been extended to virtually every form of public employment in addition to the services under the state government.

[51] *Report of the Commissioner for Scheduled Castes and Scheduled Tribes (Twenty-sixth Report), 1978–79*, Controller of Publications (Delhi), n.d., part I, p. 61.

The state of Karnataka has gone furthest in systematizing the policy of job reservation. In Karnataka University at Dharwar, 'The reservation for Scheduled Castes/Scheduled Tribes in the appointments to the teaching posts are made on the basis of the directions of the State Government from time to time. They have reserved posts for Scheduled Castes and Scheduled Tribes and backward tribals and other backward classes to the extent of 15%, 3%, 5% and 28% respectively.'[52] Thus, more than half the posts are reserved on the basis of caste and community, and, of the reserved posts, more than half are earmarked for the Other Backward Classes consisting in the main of various castes and communities.

Apart from the high proportion of teaching posts reserved for particular castes and communities, what is striking is the manner in which the universities have followed the government in its rules and procedures. After all, the universities might have gone their own way in seeking to ensure a wider representation of the various sections of society on the ground that the requirements of a university faculty are different from those of a government bureaucracy. But in many cases they have decided not to do so. *The Karnataka State Universities Act, 1976* says that, in making recommendations for appointments, 'the Board shall follow the orders issued by the State Government from time to time in the matter of reservation of posts for the Scheduled Castes, the Scheduled Tribes and other backward classes of citizens'. Similarly, *The Kerala University Act* of 1974 lays down that in making appointments to both teaching and non-teaching posts the university must observe the provisions of the Kerala State and Subordinate Services Rules in regard to the reservation of posts.

Among the states of northern India, Bihar followed for several years the practice of making university appointments through the State Public Service Commission. The Public Service Commissions enjoy a certain authority in India by virtue of their reputation for fairness and impartiality. The Bihar Public Service Commission was called into use in making academic appointments after the normal machinery in the universities had fallen into disrepute because of widespread allegations of corruption and nepotism. But the regular use of the Public Service Commission must lead in the end to the displacement of the requirements of academic discrimination by those of administrative or procedural uniformity.

[52] Ibid., part II, p. 27.

Government service enjoys high prestige in India, and there are certain conditions of government service, such as security of tenure and regularity of promotions, that have a large if not universal appeal among university teachers. University teachers in India enjoy virtually the same measure of security as government officials, but the prospects of promotion are different in the two cases. When university teachers compare themselves with gazetted officers in government service, they find that, although they start on broadly the same salary, their prospects of moving into higher salary grades are much smaller. Thus, the demand for 'meaningful avenues of promotion' has gathered strength among university lecturers in all parts of the country. This demand is accompanied by a jealous and watchful eye for cases where the claims of seniority are overlooked when lecturers move to readerships, or readers to professorships.

In effect the overwhelming sentiment among university and college lecturers is that there should be more room for promotion and that promotion should be by seniority:[53] in that way all who succeed in entering the university service as lecturers at the same time will have equal chances of becoming readers. Here again, the universities in Bihar have taken a lead by deciding that all lecturers will automatically become readers after thirteen years of service if they have Ph.D. degrees and after eighteen years if they do not. This reflects not so much a commitment to equality as the urge for security and a safe upward passage of those with their feet on the first rung of the ladder. The state may subsidise upward mobility to a certain extent, but even in this its role is strictly limited in an economy of scarcity. To what extent this kind of subsidized mobility can create equality of condition or simulate equality of opportunity is a different question altogether.

[53] A well-known Indian academic has recently written, 'Teachers' unions all over the country demand that their salary scales be raised, that they should have automatic promotion without any selection procedures and that all temporary lecturers should be confirmed in their posts.' Daya Krishna, 'India's Liberal Democracy', *The Times of India*, New Delhi, 15 June 1981.

Equality of Opportunity

The G. L. Mehta Memorial Lecture, 1982

Our age, it is said, is the age of equality. This does not mean that the inequalities deposited by the past have ceased to exist or that no new inequalities can be expected to arise. But it does mean perhaps that people no longer accept inequality in social life as a matter of course. For every inequality that persists or is likely to arise, people now want a reason, and the reasons that sufficed in the past are no longer found sufficient. On the other hand, no specific reason seems to be required for treating all persons equally. 'The assumption is', as Isaiah Berlin put it in a well-known essay on the subject, 'that equality needs no reason, only inequality does so.'[1]

Even a hundred years ago people were not prepared to concede as much to equality as they are now prepared to do. John Stuart Mill observed in the middle of the last century that his countrymen found 'the very idea of equality strange and offensive'.[2] His contemporary, Walter Bagehot the constitutionalist, defended the reverence for rank, especially hereditary rank, finding it more healthy than the reverence for either wealth or office.[3] But a change in people's consciousness had already set in, and it did not take very long for the new consciousness to make inroads even among people long accustomed, like the Indians, to accepting an unusually hierarchical society as a part of the natural scheme of things.[4]

[1] Isaiah Berlin, *Concepts and Categories: Philosophical Essays*, The Hogarth Press, 1978, p. 84.

[2] Quoted in Keith Joseph and Jonathan Sumption, *Equality*, John Murray, 1979, p. 12.

[3] Walter Bagehot, *The English Constitution*, Oxford University Press, 1928 (first published 1867), p. 81.

[4] This consciousness is very much in evidence in the writings of Bengali intellectuals of the nineteenth century from Rammohan Roy to Bankimchandra Chatterji. There is Bankim's well-known essay on equality, 'Samya', published just over a hundred years ago as well as other essays by him, notably the

Now, it is one thing to expose the arbitrariness of the inequalities contained in existing institutional arrangements, but quite another to institute equality by an act of collective will. The gap between what may be called the critical and the constructive sides of equality bedevils students of society everywhere, but nowhere more insistently than in India today. Nothing seems to be more easy than to expose the arbitrary, not to say perverse, nature of the inequalities deposited by successive historical epochs on Indian society; and nothing more difficult than to create conditions that will ensure equal enjoyment of even the barest necessities of life.

The traditional order of Indian society was notoriously hierarchical, although by no means uniquely so. Like most of the contemporary world, Indian society too is now oriented towards the goal of equality. In changing its orientation from hierarchy to equality, India was no doubt following the example of the West. When Indians experienced a sustained exposure to Western values for the first time in the middle of the nineteenth century, the West was turning its back on its own traditional hierarchy. The traditional hierarchy soon lost credibility in India as well, and Indians began to champion the cause of equality, particularly in their dealings with their European masters.[5] Given the fact that Indians had lived with the hierarchy of caste for two thousand years, it is remarkable what little effort they made to put forward any sustained intellectual defence of it; turning, instead, to the invention of a past in which equality could be shown to be the governing principle of collective life.

Despite the historical connection, there are certain important differences between the Indian transition from a hierarchical to an egalitarian orientation and the one accomplished earlier in the West. The traditional hierarchy was more rigid and elaborate, and enjoyed greater stability in India than it did in the West; whereas the public commitment to equality is more sweeping in India today than it was in the corresponding period in the West. Moreover, the transition from the old to the new ideology took place over a much longer period of time in the West than in India, and, what is more important,

one on 'Self-rule and Alien rule'. These writings as well as others of that period are discussed in an illuminating study by B. N. Ganguli, *Concept of Equality: The Nineteenth Century Indian Debate*, Indian Institute of Advanced Study (Simla), 1975.

[5] Ibid.

under material conditions that were far more conducive to making the ideal of equality real than anything that has prevailed in India during the last hundred years. In the West the ideal of equality became socially established at a time when material wealth was expanding rapidly enough to allow, if not to encourage, a degree of redistribution among persons. In India the very limited growth of material wealth, particularly in relation to the growth of population, makes the problem of redistribution enormously more complex and difficult.

The contrast between the two patterns of transition brings us to a distinction of great importance between two aspects of inequality. There is, firstly, the inequality inherent in a structure of privileges and disabilities created or protected by law, characteristic of societies arranged in a hierarchy of estates or castes. But underlying this, and separate from it, is the inequality of life chances whose structure is governed largely, though by no means solely, by the size and distribution of material resources. The first aspect of inequality is characteristic of only some societies; the second is universal.

The first advance towards equality in the modern age was made when society moved from a legal order based on a series of privileges and disabilities to one based on a mutuality of rights and obligations. On the continent of Europe it was this change that the French Revolution dramatized. In England the same change took place, but less dramatically and over a longer period of time. The traditional hierarchy had not been as rigid or as elaborate as in France and some residues of it still survive, as for instance in the monarchy and the hereditary peerage.

In writing about medieval England, the legal historian Maitland contrasted ordinary or common persons—'free and lawful men' as he called them—with all others who either enjoyed privileges or were subject to disabilities.[6] In the traditional order of Hindu society, 'free and lawful men' in Maitland's sense were uncommon; for the better part, they either enjoyed privileges or were subject to disabilities. Notable among these were the ones built into the relations between the various castes and between the sexes.[7] The Hindu *Dharma-*

[6] Frederick Pollock and Frederic William Maitland, *The History of English Law before the Time of Edward I*, Cambridge University Press, second edition, 1968, vol. 1, p. 407.

[7] B. Sivaramayya, 'Equality and Inequality in the Legal System' in A. Béteille (ed.), *Equality and Inequality*, Oxford University Press, 1983.

shastras dwell upon the disabilities of the Shudras and of women extensively and in detail.

The privileges and disabilities of the traditional social order came under severe attack from the middle of the nineteenth century onwards both from the British rulers of India and from Western-educated Indians, and they had lost much of their legitimacy by the time the country became independent in 1947. The new Constitution, adopted in 1950, sought to erase all traditional privileges and disabilities, and to establish full equality of status: untouchability was abolished and legal equality was established between castes and between the sexes. The courts have in the last thirty years upheld the equality provisions of the Constitution and have, if anything, amplified and extended them. But there has been no appreciable advance of equality in the distribution of wealth and income in the corresponding period to match the advance of legal equality.[8]

If by status we mean a set of rights and obligations created and protected by law, equality of status cannot by any means be said to guarantee equality of condition by which we might mean equality in the enjoyment of all the things that men and women value in a society. Equality of status may be necessary for attaining equality of condition, but it is not sufficient for it. Indeed, some would question that it is at all possible to create, not merely in real life but even in the imagination, all the prerequisites of full equality of condition among men and women.[9]

There are those who question not only the possibility of equality of condition but also its desirability, and yet it cannot be said that they are necessarily opposed to equality as such; for they may be strong advocates of equality of opportunity. One might indeed argue that all that we need for a healthy and a just society are equality of status and equality of opportunity, and that equality of condition is neither attainable nor desirable; and, further, that all attempts to attain it lead sooner or later to a sacrifice of either liberty or efficiency, or both.

[8] Compare the contribution by Sivaramayya with the one by S. D. Tendulkar in Béteille (ed.), *Equality and Inequality*.

[9] See the essay entitled 'Equality' by Isaiah Berlin in his *Concepts and Categories*; see also Talcott Parsons, 'A Revised Analytical Approach to the Theory of Social Stratification' in Reinhard Bendix and Seymour Martin Lipset (eds.), *Class, Status and Power: A Reader in Social Stratification*, The Free Press, 1953, pp. 92–128.

Equality of oportunity may thus be presented as a workable compromise between social ideals and material realities. Acceptance of it marks an undeniable advance over a state in which individuals belonging to particular castes, creeds or races, or to one particular sex are *in principle* excluded from positions of respect and responsibility. In India, where the principle of exclusion had been carried to its outer limit, the general acceptance of equality of opportunity involves a departure of some significance from the traditional order of things. At the same time, equality of opportunity does not try to eliminate social distinctions as such; it tries only to enable individuals to achieve distinction according to their merits.

It has been argued that the very idea of equality of opportunity or even of opportunity itself is a modern one, inconceivable in past societies in which families occupied fixed stations in life. 'The fixed stations in life which most families occupied precluded any idea of "opportunity", and even less [sic], equality of opportunity.'[10] This argument draws attention to an important distinction, although we must not exaggerate the extent to which individuals and families were fixed in their stations in even the most traditional societies of the past.

The Preamble to the Indian Constitution speaks of the resolve to secure 'equality of status and of opportunity'. Now, equality of status and of opportunity may be legally instituted under conditions of little or no material change in a society. In that case a few individuals with exceptional ability or unusual good luck might rise to positions of distinction by overcoming the adversity of social circumstances. But for the vast majority of individuals no substantial change of social position will be likely to occur as a result of the change in the legal order. The structure of unequal life chances established under the old legal order will be carried over into the new one, despite the abolition of privileges and disabilities till then guaranteed by the law.

In the West throughout the eighteenth and nineteenth centuries large changes were in fact taking place in the economy which altered the structure of life chances by creating new opportunities not just for a few isolated individuals but for large numbers of them. New wealth was being created on an unprecedented scale and, side by side with it, a new occupational structure. In the industrial countries of the West the new occupational structure now dominates society to

[10] James Coleman, 'The Concept of Equality of Educational Opportunity', *Harvard Educational Review*, vol. 38, no. 1, Winter 1968, p. 8.

an extent unexampled in the past. The social identity of the individual has come to be defined largely, if not primarily, by his occupation in an office or a factory: much of his adult life turns around it and his early life is mainly a preparation for it. It is within this occupational structure that the concept of equality of opportunity acquired much of its significance.

The new occupational structure found it easier to accommodate the principle of equal opportunity than any that had existed in the past. It favoured recruitment by competition over recruitment by birth in the interest of efficiency of performance which came to be more and more strictly, not to say narrowly, assessed. Moreover, it was inherently dynamic, creating for every new generation a large number of positions to be filled by individuals with uncommon ability or unusual luck, or both.[11]

What fixed the family to its station in life in past societies was not merely the idea of fidelity to a given way of life but also the fact that new occupations, hence new stations in life, grew very slowly if at all in such societies. Today, on the other hand, we have not only a new idea, namely, that each individual must find his own station in life, but also the fact that the economy through its own inherent dynamism generates new occupations with unexampled rapidity. It is impossible to consider the creation of new opportunities today without considering the creation of new occupations. Thus, in a country like India, 'the opening of opportunities to individuals' will depend not merely on the commitment to equality as an ideal but also on what can be teased out of the economy.

The idea of careers open to talent, which gained currency in revolutionary France, called for a radical change in the educational system and, in particular, a closer co-ordination between it and the emerging occupational structure. Here again, the French took the lead by setting up a system of *grandes écoles* outside the university faculties, weighed down as they were by their medieval hierarchies and privileges. The two most famous among these, the École

---

[11] There is a vast literature on occupational structure and social mobility in the West. For a recent general essay, written in a provocative style, see Ernest Gellner, 'The Social Roots of Egalitarianism', *Dialectics and Humanism*, vol. 4, 1979. A standard reference book is Reinhard Bendix and Seymour Martin Lipset (eds.), *Class, Status and Power: Social Stratification in Comparative Perspective*, The Free Press, second edition, 1966, especially section V, 'Social Mobility'. A more recent work with an excellent bibliography is John H. Goldthorpe, *Social Mobility and Class Structure in Modern Britain*, Clarendon Press, 1980.

Polytechnique set up in 1794 to train engineers for the civil and military services, and the École Normale Supérieure set up in 1795 to train teachers for state secondary schools, recruited students through stiff but open competition.[12] The open competitive examination became in course of time an essential complement of higher education and training all over the world, aligning these with the capitalist enterprise on the one hand and the apparatus of government on the other.[13]

Not surprisingly, when the first three universities were established in India in the middle of the last century, they started with examining rather than teaching. At the present time when in India university education as a whole seems to be collapsing under the weight of the examination system, it is well to remember that, historically, recruitment by open competitive examination was designed to replace recruitment by birth and patronage.[14] The new system appealed instantly to Indians with ambition and enterprise; and, where they

[12] For a general and very readable account of higher education in France from mid-nineteenth to mid-twentieth century, see the chapter on 'Universities' in Theodore Zeldin, *France 1848–1945*, vol. 2, Clarendon Press, 1977. A good recent study in English of one of the two principal *grandes écoles* is Robert J. Smith, *The École Normale Supérieure and the Third Republic*, State University of New York Press, 1982.

[13] The link between modern educational institutions and the modern occupational structure through competitive examinations has been underlined by many. Max Weber wrote, 'Educational institutions on the European continent, especially the institutions of higher learning—the universities, as well as technical academies, business colleges, gymnasia, and other secondary schools—, are dominated and influenced by the need for the kind of "education" which is bred by the system of specialized examinations or tests of expertise (*Fachprufungwesen*) increasingly indispensable for modern bureaucracies.' Further, 'Only the modern development of full bureaucratization brings the system of rational examinations for expertise irresistibly to the fore.' And, finally, 'The bureaucratization of capitalism, with its demand for expertly trained technicians, clerks, etc., carries such examinations all over the world.' (Max Weber, *Economy and Society*, University of California Press, 1978, vol. 2, pp. 999–1000).

[14] Zeldin writes about the universities in pre-Revolutionary France: 'Many professors had abandoned lecturing altogether, and confined themselves to the lucrative task of issuing degrees. . . . Examinations were more a financial than an academic matter, in fact the purchase of a privilege.' (Zeldin, *France 1848–1945*, vol. 2, p. 316). Oxford in the eighteenth century had an examination system that was no less lax or corrupt; see Sheldon Rothblatt, 'The Student Sub-culture and Examination System in Early 19th Century Oxbridge' in Lawrence Stone (ed.), *The University in Society*, Princeton University Press, 1974, vol. 1, pp. 267–303.

could not prepare to take competitive examinations themselves, they turned to preparing their children to take them.

Opportunities began to open and to expand for educated Indians in the professions and the services where examination results counted for more than did caste, at least for those who were successful: those who failed could believe, not altogether without reason, that their social background had gone against them. It is difficult to say how much confidence there was in the system in its early phase and among which sections of society: its capacity to meet the expectations it created was never very large, never nearly as large in India as in Britain or France, not to speak of the United States, the true land of opportunity in the nineteenth century.

With the simultaneous increase in the pressure for higher education and in unemployment among the educated, the disjunction between the expectations created by the new system and its capacity to satisfy them has quickly come to the surface. This disjunction forces on our attention the distinction between equality of opportunity and equality of result.[15] Equality of opportunity can mean something only in a system based on competition. But competition, even when fully free and open, cannot ensure equality of result: indeed, the object of competition, whether in education or in employment, is to secure not equality of result but its opposite.

If then we insist on equality of opportunity, we must be prepared for inequality of result, whether in America or in India. But the results need not show identically the same pattern of inequality everywhere. The extent to which the new pattern of inequality created by competition departs from the old pattern existing before it varies greatly from one case to another. There is some evidence to show that competition not only entails inequality of result but that it reproduces existing inequalities to a large extent even in advanced industrial societies such as France.[16]

Much patience and care are required for analysing systematically the patterns in the inequality created, under varying initial conditions, by competition on the basis of equal opportunity. Attempts

[15] See James S. Coleman, 'Equality of Opportunity and Equality of Results', *Harvard Educational Review*, vol. 43, no. 1, February 1973, pp. 129–37.

[16] Pierre Bourdieu and Jean-Claude Passeron, *Reproduction in Education, Society and Culture*, Sage Publications, 1977.

have been made to account for these patterns by a variety of factors of which three seem to be of particular importance. These may be briefly described as (i) natural endowment, (ii) social circumstance and (iii) luck or chance. In the discussion that follows I shall be concerned mainly with the second of these factors, briefly with the first, and hardly at all with the third.

To take up the first point first. It may be argued that inequality of result will necessarily follow from equality of opportunity because of the unequal distribution of natural endowment among persons. This argument questions the proposition that 'all men are created equal'; or treats it as a convenient fiction; or maintains that the proposition might apply to civic or political rights but not to merit or ability or talent. As I have argued elsewhere, the belief in natural inequality is very deeply rooted among men, and not least in the contemporary Western democracies.[17]

The idea of natural inequality, though an old one, was given new scientific underpinnings in the nineteenth century, particularly by biologists and psychologists. Among the pioneers in the field was the English scientist and explorer Sir Francis Galton who maintained that human intelligence was both unequally distributed and hereditarily transmitted,[18] and in course of time laid the foundation of the new science of eugenics. It is said that Galton converted his celebrated cousin Sir Charles Darwin to his viewpoint on human intelligence, and another well-known English biologist, T. H. Huxley —'Darwin's bulldog', as he called himself—also stressed the significance of unequal natural endowment.[19] These theories of natural inequality have enabled many to argue that the inequalities actually existing in their society are a necessary, if not desirable, consequence of the equality of opportunity.

The argument about natural inequality is easiest to make for a population that is biologically differentiated in an obvious way as, for instance, when it is divided into different races or between

[17] André Béteille, *The Idea of Natural Inequality*, republished in this volume, pp. 7–32.

[18] Francis Galton, *Hereditary Genius*, Watts, second edition, 1950 (first published 1869), ushered in a new era in the use of scientific methods to explain and justify the presence of inequalities in societies unencumbered by legal privileges and disabilities. Galton and men of his temper opposed 'privilege' as strongly as they endorsed 'genius'.

[19] T. H. Huxley, 'On the Natural Inequality of Men', *The Nineteenth Century*, no. 155, 1890, pp. 1–23.

men and women. Actually, in the nineteenth century even in America, few people seriously believed that the doctrine of equality of opportunity was intended to cover Negroes or women.[20] American attitudes to women have altered vastly, although the idea of the inherent inferiority of the Negro remains deeply ingrained.[21] Even in the nineteenth century, although both were largely excluded from the arena of public competition, the reasons or the prejudices responsible for their exclusion were not of the same kind; just as in traditional India, where both women and Shudras were subject to disabilities, the disabilities were very different in the two cases.

Remarkable changes have taken place during the last hundred years in the social position of middle-class women not only in the West but also in India. These changes show that inferior performance may be due less to natural inferiority than to social prejudice or lack of motivation, or some combination of the two. It may be due as well to lack of means. If women still perform poorly in competition relatively to men, as they generally do, it is often because they lack the resources rather than the abilities for successful competition. The same argument holds true, by and large, for unequal performance by members of different castes and, perhaps, also of different races.

The plain fact is that there are vast differences of social circumstance in even the most advanced of modern societies and even among male members of the same race, and these make it difficult to talk about ensuring equality in the external conditions of competition. This point was forcefully made in a well-known book on equality published fifty years ago by the English socialist R. H.

[20] For an excellent recent account by an English historian of American attitudes in the nineteenth century to equality, including attitudes to Negroes and women, see J. R. Pole, *The Pursuit of Equality in American History*, University of California Press, 1978.

[21] There is of course a great deal of evidence to show that the scholastic achievements of Negroes are consistently below those of Whites. While it is true that not all those who seek to account for this evidence by genetic factors are prejudiced, many, if not most, are. It seems to me that American attitudes towards the biological aspects of race have altered very little in the last hundred years, although the language in which these attitudes are expressed has. See, for instance, the special number of *Harvard Educational Review*, vol. 43, no. 1, February 1973, devoted to a discussion of the work by Jencks; also, vol. 39, nos. 1, 2, and 3 (Winter, Spring and Summer 1969) of the same journal carrying the essay by Jensen, 'How Much Can We Boost IQ and Scholastic Achievement?' and a discussion of it.

Tawney.[22] Tawney's argument raises serious misgivings about equality of opportunity from the egalitarian position itself.

Tawney drew attention to the disparities in social circumstance that, especially in England, survived the abolition of legal privileges and disabilities, and continued to affect unequally the chances of success in competition of individuals belonging to different social classes.[23] He was particularly critical of the social conditions prevailing in England which, following Matthew Arnold fifty years before him, he compared unfavourably with those in other European countries and in the United States. What Tawney said of England fifty years ago can be said with greater force about India today where large inequalities in the distribution of life chances continue to exist despite the creation of the most extensive legal equality.

Legal equality may be necessary to give everybody some chance in the competition for positions of respect and responsibility, but it is by no means sufficient. To put it in Tawney's well-chosen words:

> In reality, of course, except in a sense which is purely formal, equality of opportunity is not simply a matter of legal equality. Its existence depends, not merely on the absence of disabilities, but on the presence of abilities. It obtains in so far as, and only in so far as, each member of a community, whatever his birth, or occupation, or social position, possesses in fact, and not merely in form, equal chances of using to the full his natural endowments of physique, of character, and of intelligence.[24]

Tawney goes on to argue that it makes very little sense to talk of distributing rewards according to capacity when it is well known that the capacities of some are 'sterilized or stunted' and of others 'favoured or pampered' by their social environment.

Tawney's arguments cut very deep. For they lead to questions not merely about existing conditions in English or Indian society, but about the very possibility of establishing 'real' as opposed to 'formal' equality of opportunity. How are we to ensure that every member of the community has equal chances of using to the full all his natural endowments without first creating equality of condition?

[22] R. H. Tawney, *Equality*, Unwin Books, new edition, 1964 (first published 1931).

[23] Tawney's misgivings about the unequal life chances of individuals belonging to different social classes have been amply borne out by studies of social mobility made in Britain since his time. See Goldthorpe, *Social Mobility and Class Structure in Modern Britain*.

[24] Tawney, *Equality*, pp. 103–4.

12

And, if we can create equality of condition and maintain it for successive generations, what need will there be for equality of opportunity? It is in this light that we must view the recent observation of a distinguished American educationist that 'the ideal of equal opportunity is a false ideal'.[25]

Equality of opportunity remains illusory when inequalities of condition are all-embracing, and there is no longer any need for it when they disappear altogether. It might appear tempting in view of this to abandon the slow pursuit of equality of opportunity in favour of a quick and decisive exercise of the collective will to establish equality of condition at one stroke. But equality of condition has never been established in that way or in any other way and, even if so established, it is difficult to see how it can be sustained within the regime of scarcity that is the common lot of all human societies. Too many other values, such as liberty and efficiency, will have to be sacrificed if not abandoned in the effort to secure equality of condition.

It follows that we cannot, despite its many limitations, dispense with equality of opportunity, especially in India, and it is therefore important to see where these limitations lie, and how and to what extent they may be remedied. Now, while we have to distinguish analytically between equality of opportunity and equality of condition, it would be wrong, not to say disingenuous, to discuss the one in isolation from the other. Especially in societies which have inherited from the past severe inequalities in the distribution of life chances, equality of opportunity can advance very little without some *independent* advance being made in equality of condition by imposing limits through social intervention on both the rewards and the penalties of competition.

Those who assign overriding importance to competition in the name of equality of opportunity may be criticized on two grounds. Firstly, it may be wrong to attribute success or failure in competition solely or even mainly to natural endowment without paying due attention to social circumstance or to chance. Secondly, it may be wrong to encourage or to tolerate extremes in the distribution of rewards and penalties even where it can be established that success and failure are due entirely to differences of natural endowment. There is nothing in the natural distribution of talents that can itself

[25] Coleman, 'Equality of Opportunity and Equality of Results', p. 135; see also his 'Equality of Educational Opportunity'.

determine in what proportion success should be rewarded and failure penalized.

Untempered competition between individuals has consequences not only for the members of society considered as individuals but also for the institutional order of society. Western societies have accepted the principle of competition as the norm in most institutional spheres, particularly those of work, but even under capitalism in its most unrestrained form, one institutional sphere, i.e. the home, was expected to be governed by a different norm.[26] Competition between colleagues in the office was considered one thing; competition at home between spouses or between siblings, particularly of opposite sex, quite another.[27] These attitudes are now changing as the logic of equality becomes extended to the relations between men and women. It is difficult to see how far the demand for full equality of opportunity between the sexes can be met without dislocation of what has been probably the most durable institution invented by man, namely, the family. But the family, which has been the seedbed of discrimination between the sexes, has also been among social institutions the one pre-eminently responsible for the nurture and care of all its individual members, irrespective of merit or talent.[28]

I have already indicated that some people argue that it is unjust to carry rewards and penalties to extremes where success and failure are due to accidents of social circumstance rather than differences of natural endowment, while others go further and insist that such extremes cannot be justified even where success and failure are due entirely to differences of natural endowment. There are fundamental differences between the two viewpoints which may be contrasted as the meritarian and the human points of view. According to the

[26] The institutional polarization between work and home in American society is discussed with great clarity in Talcott Parsons et al., *Family, Socialization and Interaction Process*, The Free Press, 1955. See also David M. Schneider, *American Kinship: A Cultural Account*, Prentice-Hall, 1968.

[27] This is not to suggest that there is *in fact* no strife within the bosom of the family. The undercurrent of hostility between family members has been the staple fare of studies by psychoanalysts. See R. D. Laing, *The Politics of the Family and Other Essays*, Tavistock Publications, 1971.

[28] The moral basis of kinship has been elucidated by many anthropologists, but by none more cogently than Meyer Fortes. See his *Kinship and the Social Order*, Routledge and Kegan Paul, 1970, especially chapter 12, 'Kinship and the Axiom of Amity'. For a more general account of the two sides of the family—the nurture of all and the discrimination between the sexes—see D. H. J. Morgan, *Social Theory and the Family*, Routledge and Kegan Paul, 1975.

latter, all human beings are entitled to certain things, including dignity and respect, as human beings and irrespective of differences of race, caste, creed, sex—and intelligence. The minimal equality of condition that this requires should be given priority over any scheme of differential rewards and penalties.[29] The analogy of the family, as it has been till now, is sometimes used in justifying the application of the human point of view as against the meritarian, at least by those who would like to see less emphasis placed on equality of opportunity.[30]

The aristocratic or hierarchical point of view which prevailed in the past paid attention to distinctions of social circumstance in every sphere of life. The meritarian point of view emphasizes distinctions of natural endowment as against those of social circumstance, regarding the latter as arbitrary or accidental. According to the human point of view, both kinds of distinction are to some extent accidental, so that too much importance should not be attached to either.

The question of the moral significance of disparities of natural endowment has been sharply posed by the American philosopher John Rawls. Rawls has been at pains to point out the equal arbitrariness, from the moral point of view, of the influence on distributive shares of social contingencies and of natural chance. It is now widely accepted that individuals should not benefit unduly from the accidents of social circumstance, such as being born in a comfortable home. How far should they be allowed to benefit from the natural lottery which gives them at birth unusual physical or mental endowments? As Rawls puts it, 'There is no more reason to permit the distribution of income and wealth to be settled by the distribution of natural assets than by historical and social fortune.'[31] For, he goes on to add, 'no one deserves his place in the distribution of

[29] This viewpoint is presented very persuasively by Bernard Williams, 'The Idea of Equality' in P. Laslett and W. G. Runciman (eds.), *Politics, Philosophy and Society*, second series, Basil Blackwell, 1964, pp. 110–31.

[30] Coleman writes in 'Equality of Opportunity and Equality of Results', 'A society cannot make an implementable decision to create equal opportunity for all children within it. . . . Indeed, this is what families themselves do with their different children who are differentially endowed . . . They do not aim for, nor do they end up with, equality of opportunity, but instead a reduced inequality of opportunity among their children' (p. 135).

[31] John Rawls, *A Theory of Justice*, Oxford University Press, 1972, p. 74.

native endowments, any more than one deserves one's initial starting place in society.'[32]

Similar questions tend to be raised by educationists when they find that, contrary to their own expectations, genetic endowment does significantly influence scholastic achievement. Students of education, particularly in America, are now coming to realize that it might be a futile endeavour to try to eliminate inequality through equality of opportunity because competition as such might increase rather than reduce inequality, if only through the mechanism of genetic selection. And Christopher Jencks, the author of an influential study in this area, has concluded in the same vein as Rawls: 'For a thoroughgoing egalitarian, however, inequality that derives from biology ought to be as repulsive as inequality that derives from early socialization.'[33]

The 'thoroughgoing egalitarian' may not be able to derive great comfort from the world as it exists in reality. This reality requires us to either qualify the principle of equality of opportunity pure and simple or to use it in combination with some other principle in order to move towards what Tawney had described as 'practical equality'.

Rawls has sought to oppose to the principle of equality of opportunity pure and simple—which in his mind is associated with the idea of careers open to talent and with a callous meritocratic society —what he describes as 'fair equality of opportunity', or 'equality of fair opportunity'. To speak of fair equality of opportunity is to mean in a broad sense that 'those with similar abilities and skills should have similar life chances'.[34] Where people are favoured with abilities and skills, the accident of social circumstance should not be allowed to deprive them of the opportunity to use these to their advantage. Nor should every opportunity be closed to them even where natural chance has given them only a meagre allotment of skills and abilities.

Using slightly different terminology, and specifically in the context of education, Jencks contrasts 'equal opportunity' with what he calls 'compensatory opportunity'. Compensatory opportunity means helping the neediest whereas equal opportunity means treating everyone alike. Jencks insists on the need to recognize the distinction between the two, although he is himself sceptical about the extent to

---

[32] Ibid., p. 104.
[33] Christopher Jencks, *Inequality*, Penguin Books, 1975, p. 73.
[34] Rawls, *A Theory of Justice*, p. 73.

which compensatory opportunity can within the existing school system bring about greater equality in performance beyond the school. And he concludes that 'even if we reorganised the schools so that their primary concern was for the students who most needed help, there is no reason to suppose that adults would end up appreciably more equal as a result'.[35]

The arguments of social theorists from Tawney to Rawls have made us sensitive to the social costs of carrying to extremes the rewards and penalties of untempered competition. At the same time, we must not think that a comprehensive system of compensatory opportunities will be without any social costs. Where poor performance is due to neither unfavourable social circumstance nor inadequate natural endowment, but to sheer lack of effort, it would clearly be both unjust and inefficient to offer compensation or redress in the name of fair equality of opportunity. The problem arises because it is difficult to exclude from the definition of ability the ability for sustained effort; and, while it might appear reasonable to compensate people for lack of ability, it would be paradoxical, not to say quixotic, to reward them for lack of effort.[36]

We cannot overlook the thread which links equality *via* individualism to an activist orientation to the social order. If a regime of castes or of estates requires the individual to resign himself to his allotted place in society, a system of classes allows and indeed encourages him to move from one position to another. There is no doubt that in the modern world the zest for equality has owed a great deal to the prospects as well as the hazards of social mobility. But then that zest is destroyed not only where mobility is made so easy as to become unnecessary but also where it is so difficult as to remain impossible.

The discussion of equality has acquired a much wider scope in the second half of the twentieth century than it had in the nineteenth. Many of the issues then ignored or overlooked—such as those relating to women or to stigmatized minorities—have now become

---

[35] Jencks, *Inequality*, p. 255.

[36] For a discussion which relates 'opportunity' to 'effortful activity' on the basis of a distinction between 'chance' and 'opportunity', see T. D. Campbell, 'Equality of Opportunity', *Proceedings of the Aristotelian Society*, new series, vol. 75, 1975, pp. 51–68.

important. The problems of creating equality for them—whether equality of condition or equality of opportunity—are of a different order from those of creating equality for artisans or peasants or workers, or even servants. It may be said without too much exaggeration that in Europe and America these problems have on the whole emerged sequentially whereas in India they have more or less all come up together: a quick look at the Directive Principles of State Policy will give some idea of the range of issues to which the makers of the Constitution of India had to attend simultaneously.

Nineteenth-century ideas of equality no doubt appeared revolutionary in the light of the conditions that had existed under the *ancien régime*; but we today are struck as much by the claims to equality—actual or potential—that were denied, ignored or overlooked throughout the nineteenth century and well into the twentieth. We have to think only of the Negroes in America and of women in both Europe and America to realize that there was denial not merely of equality of condition and of opportunity, but also of legal equality, including what today would be considered as the basic rights of citizenship. This denial has left marks on the distribution of life chances that are only too apparent in the contemporary world.

What is striking about the advocates of equality in the nineteenth century is that so many of them thought that equality was around the corner or that considerable progress had been made towards its attainment in some country other than their own. Tocqueville, the French aristocrat, argued that America was showing the road to equality to the rest of the world; yet we know that in America the Negroes suffered from the most cruel denial of rights in Tocqueville's lifetime and after. The Englishman Matthew Arnold (and after him R. H. Tawney) maintained that the French had progressed much further than the English on the road to equality,[37] yet we know that in France women got the right to vote only in 1944 towards the end of a long and exhausting war.

'The French Revolution', it has been said, 'established not so much equality as the principle of equality of opportunity, which meant that competitiveness was raised into a virtue.'[38] Even that statement has to be taken with many reservations. The outcome of the competitiveness, as we now know, was the creation of a mandarinate.

[37] Matthew Arnold, *Mixed Essays*, John Murray, 1903 (popular edition), pp. 48–97.
[38] Zeldin, *France 1848–1945*, vol. 2, p. 1157.

As the mandarinate consolidated itself, it became increasingly apparent that, although entry into it was wide open in principle, it was severely restricted in practice. Leaving aside altogether the question of women—after taking note of the sentiment that a woman was expected to benefit from the success of her husband or her sons—it is quite clear that equality of opportunity was to a large extent refracted by the class structure of society—its division, for example, into capitalists, managers, officials, workers, artisans, peasants, etc.

The refraction of equal opportunity becomes even more manifest when we add to disadvantaged classes, such as peasants, artisans and workers, disprivileged categories and groups, such as women and stigmatized minorities whose members were until recently debarred from the competition in principle as well as in practice. Where the accumulation of disadvantages has been long and sustained, the case for redress would appear to be both just and reasonable. The principle of redress has become established as a part of the contemporary consciousness in the same way in which the principle of equal opportunity had been in the nineteenth century. It is advocated in a variety of forms and it has come to be known by various names: compensatory action, protective discrimination, affirmative action, and so on. It has to be emphasized that it is designed not to cancel out the principle of equal opportunity, but to make the consequences of that principle more consistent with its intention. It is in this spirit that Rawls connects the principle of redress with the principle of fair equality of opportunity.

Considered in the abstract, the scope for redress is very wide and far-reaching. It would clearly be impossible to neutralize every disadvantage, whether of social circumstance or of natural endowment. The principle of redress, if it is to be translated into effective social action, cannot be applied piecemeal, to each case according to its individual merit. It must be applied to whole categories of persons identified by readily recognizable criteria. Much disagreement centres around the kinds of criteria to be used for this purpose and the weightages assigned to them. What prevails is not necessarily what is socially most just but what is politically most feasible for a given time and place.

Are we to regard all very poor people as handicapped, or all people belonging to a socially stigmatized minority such as the Negroes or the Harijans? The variations of natural endowment between individual members would be quite large and probably of the same order in both types of category. There would also be some variation of social circumstance within each category, although the nature of the variation might be different in the two cases.

It is likely that individuals with very high natural ability will be more successful in open competition if they are merely poor than if they belong to a socially stigmatized minority. The gains from superior natural endowment are more likely to be cumulative in the first case than in the second. Much would depend of course on the degree of social visibility of the minority in question, and also on the degree to which collective as opposed to individual identities count in the society as a whole. And of course it must not be forgotten that the very poor are as such stigmatized to a greater or lesser extent in most societies.

In what follows I shall ignore altogether the problems of redressing the disadvantages due clearly to natural endowment, as in the case of physical disability or mental insufficiency, and deal solely with those due to social circumstance. As I have indicated, the disadvantages of social circumstance are themselves diverse, and the principle of redress must pay attention to their diversity. Some people are at a disadvantage because they are victims of social prejudice on account of their collective identity even though, as individuals, they are materially well endowed or reasonably well endowed. Others are at a disadvantage solely because of the lack of material means, even though as individuals they do not carry any marks that invite social prejudice. Then again, the collective identity that invites social prejudice may be weakly or strongly marked. Where it is weakly marked, the principle of redress might seek in the long run to erase it altogether, as in the case of caste. Where it is strongly marked, as in the case of race or gender, such erasure may not be possible or even desirable.

Caste and race have often been compared by students of social stratification.[39] The many similarities between the Negroes in the United States and the Harijans in India become clear when we consider the deprivations suffered by them hitherto as well as the

[39] For contrasting points of view, see Louis Dumont, 'Caste, Racism and "Stratification": Reflections of a Social Anthropologist' in A. Béteille (ed.), *Social Inequality: Selected Readings*, Penguin Books, 1969, pp. 337–61 and Gerald D. Berreman, 'Race, Caste and Other Invidious Distinctions in Social Stratification', *Race*, No. 13, 1972, pp. 385–414; see also André Béteille, 'Race, Caste and Ethnic Identity', *International Social Science Journal*, vol. 23, no. 4, 1971, pp. 519–39.

claims of redress made on their behalf today. Individual members of both categories are to a far greater extent than other members of society prevented by the lack of material means from advancing themselves socially. But this is not all. Negroes and Harijans are marked out as collectivities so that individual Harijans and individual Negroes are handicapped by the prejudice against them even when, as individuals, they are better endowed materially and mentally than others.

But there are also differences between the two which need to be indicated while we proceed with the comparison. The collective identity of the Negroes is difficult, if not impossible, to erase; the Negro carries his uniform of colour wherever he goes. Moreover, any programme of social intervention designed to erase this identity would be today morally unacceptable in America to Whites as well as to Negroes.[40] It is difficult to see what moral objection there can be to the erasure of the collective identity of the Harijans as Harijans in contemporary Indian society. Protective discrimination in India, *unlike* affirmative action in America, is in fact designed to wipe out the very existence of the collective identities that invite social prejudice.[41] Indians with a commitment to equality find it easy to construct in their minds an ideal society of the future without any Untouchables in it; Americans will find it hard to leave out the Blacks from the construction of such a future society if they are serious about their commitment to equality.

Now while the programme of affirmative action commits Americans to assigning a certain priority to collective as against individual identities in regard to race—treating the Negro individual as a Negro rather than an individual—American society as a whole favours individualism as a value over collectivism. Traditional Indian society has, by contrast, favoured the collectivity—family, village, caste—over the individual, and the attention given to collective identities is

[40] See Talcott Parsons and Kenneth B. Clarke (eds.), *The Negro American*, Houghton Mifflin, 1966; also Pole, *The Pursuit of Equality in American History*, chapters 6 and 7.

[41] This viewpoint would be contested by liberal advocates of affirmative action in America. 'It is therefore the worst possible misunderstanding', writes the jurist Ronald Dworkin, 'to suppose that affirmative action programs are designed to produce a balkanized America, divided into racial and ethnic subnations.' (Ronald Dworkin, 'Why Bakke Has No Case', *The New York Review of Books*, 10 November 1977, p. 11. See also 'Reverse Discrimination' in his *Taking Rights Seriously*, Harvard University Press, 1978, pp. 223–39.)

still very pronounced in Indian society as a whole. Thus while the programme of protective discrimination itself may be committed to erasing the identities of caste and community, their continuance is likely to find strong support in the values inherited from the past.

The historical experience of the United States has shown how difficult it is to conform in practice to the ideal of 'separate and equal'.[42] 'Apartness' has generally meant inequality, whether in South Africa or in the United States.[43] But if the principle of redress seeks merely to compensate a few individuals for the disadvantage of race without touching the collective identity of the Blacks in a society dominated by Whites, how far can it go in establishing real equality of opportunity—fair equality of opportunity—between persons of different races?

The same problem of creating equality for persons who are visibly different and must at least in some sense always remain so arises in the case of women. We have only to mention the problem of women alongside that of disadvantaged minorities to realize how complex the idea of inequality is and how difficult it is to create equality of opportunity among persons unequally placed. The two kinds of inequality—between the sexes and of caste or race—have their roots in very different domains[44] of the institutional order and the kinds of intervention required for their redress will be correspondingly different.

The principal disability imposed upon women in traditional societies—or 'ancient societies', to adopt the phrase used by Maine— was their confinement to the domestic domain and their exclusion from the domain of public life. As Maitland points out, even where, as in medieval England, women enjoyed parity with men in private rights, they were completely excluded from public functions.[45] The

---

[42] I refer to the celebrated judgement given in 1954 in *Brown* v. *Board of Education*, which stated: 'Separate facilities are inherently unequal.'

[43] It hardly needs to be pointed out that Apartheid is the Afrikaans word for 'apartness'.

[44] I have adopted the concept of 'domain' and, in particular, that of 'domestic domain' from Fortes, *Kinship and the Social Order*; see also 'Introduction' by Meyer Fortes in Jack Goody (ed.), *The Developmental Cycle in Domestic Groups*, Cambridge University Press, 1958, pp. 1–14.

[45] Maitland sums up the position of women in England from the early Middle Ages till his own time thus: 'As regards private rights women are on the same level as men, though postponed in the canons of inheritance; but public functions they have none. In the camp, at the council board, on the bench, in the jury box

disabilities went much further in India than in the West and, whereas
the exclusion from public life was common to women of all strata,
their confinement to the home was more marked in the upper than
in the lower strata of society. The confinement and the exclusion have
both stood for the denial, to a greater or lesser extent, of moral
autonomy to women as independent agents entitled to make their
own choices for themselves on a level with men. No doubt this denial
has been imposed by society, but this imposition has been mediated
by the family and the kinship system rather than what is loosely
described as the class structure. The division of society—any society
—into classes, whether capitalists and workers or upper, middle and
lower classes, and its division into men and women are not mutually
inclusive, they are intersecting. The metaphor of class is being used
increasingly to describe the contemporary relations between the sexes
by the critics of capitalism, but that metaphor illuminates neither
the class structure nor the family system of capitalist society.[46]

In all historically known societies women have occupied an inferior
position to men and in all of them the seedbed of this inferiority has
been the family. There nevertheless have been important differences
between societies in the nature and extent of the inferiority imposed
on women by men, and it can be argued that these have been significantly associated with differences in the family system and in the
system of kinship and marriage in general. Recent historical studies
tend to bring out the uniqueness of the Western family even in pre-
industrial times.[47] Three of its outstanding and enduring features are,
the overwhelming preponderance of nuclear families, the high age
at marriage for both women and men, and the very small disparity

there is no place for them' (Pollock and Maitland, *The History of English Law*,
vol. 1, p. 485). And a student of Early Modern England has, paraphrasing Black-
stone, written. 'By marriage, the husband and wife became one person in law—
and that person was the husband' (Lawrence Stone, *The Family, Sex and Marriage
in England 1500-1700*, Weidenfeld and Nicolson, 1977, p. 195).

[46] See, for instance, the confused argument in a chapter entitled 'Women as a
Social Class' in an otherwise reasonable work, Morgan, *Social Theory and the
Family*.

[47] Most notable in this regard is the work of Peter Laslett and the Cambridge
Group for the History of Population and Social Structure. See Peter Laslett (ed.),
Household and Family in Past Time, Cambridge University Press, 1972. For a
somewhat different viewpoint, see Stone, *The Family, Sex and Marriage in
England 1500-1800*.

in age between the spouses:[48] the traditional upper caste Hindu family stood near the opposite extreme in all three regards. Finally, there is the important difference in the rule of marriage whose bearing on the position of women needs no emphasis: monogamy has been the universal rule in Western societies at least since their conversion to Christianity,[49] whereas all other major civilizations—Chinese, Hindu, Islamic—have allowed polygamy among the people and encouraged it among the privileged.

Women suffered from greater disabilities under Hindu law than perhaps under any other legal system. The Hindu *Dharmashastras* not only limit the rights of women but dwell at great and often unnecessary length on their various infirmities. Their exclusion from public life is complete and the confinement of their role to the domestic domain strict.[50] The institution known in Roman law as the Perpetual Tutelage of Women was, as Maine had pointed out, carried to its logical conclusion in India.[51] At the same time, women are not exposed under Hindu Law to the kind of punishment that always hangs as a threat over the conduct of the Shudras. The attitude towards women, it may be said, is protective rather than punitive, not unlike that of other traditional legal systems.[52]

[48] Peter Laslett, *Family Life and Illicit Love in Earlier Generations*, Cambridge University Press, 1977, especially chapter 1, 'Characteristics of the Western Family Considered Over Time'. See also Jean-Louis Flandrin, *Families in Former Times: Kinship, Household and Sexuality*, Cambridge University Press, 1979, for an analysis of the material from France; and Michael Mitterauer and Reinhard Sieder, *The European Family*, Basil Blackwell, 1982, for material from central Europe.

[49] This is not to suggest that Christianity admitted women to full equality with men. St Paul's famous injunction to the Ephesians was: 'Wives, submit yourselves unto your husbands, as unto the Lord. For the husband is the head of the wife, even as Christ is the head of the church; and he is the saviour of the body' (Ephesians 5: 22–23).

[50] It must be remembered the *Dharmashastras* dealt primarily with women of the upper castes, taking little note of lower caste women who had often to engage in onerous work outside their homes.

[51] 'In India', Maine wrote in 1861, 'the system survives in absolute completeness, and its operation is so strict that a Hindoo Mother frequently becomes the ward of her own sons' (H. S. Maine, *Ancient Law*, Oxford University Press, 1950, first published 1861, p. 127).

[52] For an excellent and remarkably well-balanced account of the position of women in Indian society, past and present, see *Towards Equality: Report of the Committee on the Status of Women in India*, Govt. of India, 1974. There has been

The creation of equality of status between men and women—equality in private and public law—has a long and complicated history in the West. India on the other hand moved from extreme inequality to complete equality or almost complete equality within a few decades with the establishment of the new Constitution in 1950. Since the nineteenth century the demand for effective equality for women has been associated with the claim for their employment outside the home or, more generally, for the desegregation of occupational roles between men and women. These claims have been resisted with two kinds of argument: firstly, that women do not have the same abilities as men and therefore their employment in superior occupations will reduce efficiency; and, secondly, that the home has a greater claim on a woman than she has on the prizes available outside it.[53] The second rather than the first argument is today the principal obstacle to the equalization of opportunities between the sexes.

That men and women should be differentially placed in society because of their differential responsibilities to the family was taken for granted in Europe, not to speak of India, until very recently, certainly until the end of the nineteenth century. The influential French sociologist Émile Durkheim argued in 1893 that the social functions of the sexes ought to be differentiated to ensure the strength and stability of the family.[54] He maintained that the two great psychic functions became progressively differentiated among human beings, women assuming responsibility for the emotions and men for the intellect.[55] And, he referred to statistics—bogus statistics, needless to say—to show that differences in brain size between men and women increased with the advance of civilization.[56]

---

much mystification around the glories of Indian womanhood by writers ranging from Coomaraswamy to Altekar. See, for instance, Ananda Coomaraswamy's essay, 'Status of Indian Women' in his *The Dance of Shiva: Fourteen Indian Essays*, Asia Publishing House, 1948, pp. 115–39; and A. S. Altekar, *Position of Women in Hindu Civilization: From Prehistoric Times to the Present Day*, Motilal Banrasidas, 1962.

[53] Theodore Zeldin, *France 1848–1945*, vol. 1, Oxford University Press, 1973, writes, 'The stress was on the family unit against the rights individuals claimed against it' (p. 299).

[54] Émile Durkheim, *The Division of Labour in Society*, The Free Press, 1933 (first published 1893), pp. 56–63.

[55] A similar metaphor has been commonly used in regard to race, assigning emotions to the Negroes and intellect to the Caucasoids.

[56] Durkheim, *The Division of Labour in Society*, p. 60.

Throughout the nineteenth century and well into the twentieth careers outside the home remained closed to women, effectively if not legally. The formula of 'careers open to talent' was not intended to apply to men and women alike but only to men. Admission and certification were denied to women not only by the older universities like Oxford and Cambridge in England, but also by the *grandes écoles* which were new institutions created by the Revolution in France. This must not be attributed solely to bad faith although there was that as well. In the nineteenth century people in Europe and America did believe in equality of opportunity, but behind that belief was a biological theory of human potentiality. According to this theory, it made sense to talk of equality of opportunity only for a biologically homogeneous population, and men and women—or Blacks and Whites—were, to all appearances, not biologically homogeneous.

Legal restrictions on the education and employment of women have been removed in India as well as in the West. With the removal of these restrictions, ideas about the unequal mental abilities of women have rapidly collapsed in marked contrast with the persistence of such ideas about the mental abilities of the different races. If women are today less visible and less successful at the higher levels of the occupational system, this can no longer be attributed to either legal or natural disability. They still have to contend against a considerable amount of social prejudice diffused through the very institutions responsible for their education and employment. But the single most important factor behind their less than equal performance is the lesser freedom they have within and in relation to the family.

With the abolition of legal disabilities, equality of opportunity between the sexes has meant the emancipation of women from the family and recognition of them as individuals. Throughout the nineteenth century a close link was assumed to exist between the advance of equality and individualism.[57] Equality of opportunity meant opportunity for the *individual* to escape from his estate or caste and to rise, by his own effort, above the condition into which he was

[57] The close linkage between the two has been analysed by Louis Dumont in his two books on India and on the West: *Homo Hierarchicus: The Caste System and Its Implications*, Paladin, 1972; and *From Mandeville to Marx: The Genesis and Triumph of Economic Ideology*, University of Chicago Press, 1977. 'Equality' and 'individualism' were of course linked together in the celebrated nineteenth-century writings of Alexis de Tocqueville and Henry Maine.

born. Liberal social thinkers welcomed the advance of equality and individualism to the extent that these were opposed to the traditional hierarchies of estate and caste.

While many saw the implications of the combined advance of individualism and equality for the structures of caste and estate, they did not all see its implications for the structure of the family. One person who saw these implications and formulated them with remarkable clarity was the jurist Sir Henry Maine. For him the advance of equality, especially the equality between men and women, meant above all the rise of the individual at the expense of the family as the unit of society.[58] 'The society, which once consisted of compact families', wrote Maine, 'has got extremely near to the condition in which it will consist exclusively of individuals when it has finally and completely assimilated the legal position of women to the legal position of men.'[59] Maine's argument will take us much further if we consider not merely legal equality between men and women, which is what he was mainly considering, but equality between them in every respect.

Maine saw the advance of equality and individualism as a part of the normal course of the development of Western societies— 'progressive societies', as he called them—from status to contract. The development has, in the course of the hundred odd years since Maine wrote, reached into many societies outside Europe and America, including India. Under the Constitution of India there is far greater legal equality between the sexes today than there was in England at the time Maine wrote. But these hundred years have also taught us to be more sceptical about the efficacy of laws in changing the real conditions of people.

Real changes have in fact been taking place in the position of women in India, although these are still confined to a small upper crust of society.[60] These changes are in some ways quite dramatic even though highly confined. Women followed men into the universities, the professions and the higher civil services in India soon after the establishment of each, with a far smaller time gap than in

[58] Maine, *Ancient Law*, pp. 104, 140.

[59] H. S. Maine, *Lectures on the Early History of Institutions*, John Murray, 1914 (first published 1875), pp. 326–7.

[60] *Towards Equality* gives a balanced account of these changes, particularly in chapters V and VI. See also the Huxley Memorial Lecture by M. N. Srinivasan, *The Changing Position of Indian Women*, Oxford University Press, 1978.

the West. The segregation of sex roles within the office had become firmly established in the West by the time women claimed parity with men in a serious way. In India these claims have come fairly early in the development of a modern occupational system. M. N. Srinivas has noted, 'The career woman in India is very visible and it is significant that the society at large has quietly accepted women's assumption of new roles'; and further, 'Men have accepted without protest women as their bosses in government offices, schools, colleges and universities.'[61]

The achievements of women within the modern occupational system have been very uneven. In some areas these have been spectacular, in others there are large blank patches. Among the professions, women have made considerable headway in education and medicine, but very little in law. In the three and a half decades since independence they have gained considerable ground in the higher civil service, and Indian women have a better foothold in it than women in most countries, including the economically-advanced ones. The Indian Civil Service under the British did not admit women. When its successor in independent India, the Indian Administrative Service, allowed the entry of women, they joined it in increasing numbers, taking some of the highest positions in the open competitive examinations.

On an average, women take about 10 to 12 per cent of the places in the Indian Administrative Service, going up to 20 per cent in some years. Thus, even where they are most successful, they do not by any means enjoy parity of representation with men. The successes achieved by women in the higher occupations have been accompanied by changes in the structure of the upper-middle class family, changes not only in the relations between husband and wife but also in the attitudes of parents towards their male and female children. It is as yet too early to say how far these changes will go and whether women will come to enjoy in relation to the family the same freedom as men not just in a few isolated pockets of Indian society but in large areas of it.

The nineteenth-century idea that equality, or at least equality of opportunity, can advance only by way of individualism still holds true to a large extent for equality between the sexes, although open

---

[61] Srinivas, *The Changing Position of Indian Women*, p. 21. The last is an overstatement. It is well known that as Chief Minister of Uttar Pradesh, Charan Singh had asked the Union Government not to send women I.A.S. officers to his state. See *Towards Equality*, p. 2.

to question in regard to other forms of equality. The Committee on the Status of Women in India asserted, 'The right to equality, in our view, like the right to free speech, is an individual right.'[62] Changes in the position of women as a category are likely to advance mainly through the achievements in education and employment of individual women. The recognition of women as individuals, to be treated on a level with men, will require the removal of prejudice in the domestic and the public domains rather than the provision of special opportunities for women over and above those to which they are entitled as individuals.[63]

In the case of such sections of society as the Negroes in America or the Harijans in India, the principle of redress has, on the other hand, given a new lease of life to the claims of collectivities as against those of individuals. Once again, one has to note the difference in this regard between India and the West, in particular America. In India the collective identities of caste and community have preserved much of their traditional strength and been scarcely displaced by the claims of individualism. American society has, on the other hand, placed the moral claims of the individual at the centre of public life from almost its very birth. The recognition of collective identities as a necessary step towards the creation of fair equality of opportunity represents in some sense a reversal of the emphasis on the individual which has from the beginning been associated with equality, or at least equality of opportunity, in America.

Creating equality of opportunity for individuals is by no means the same thing as equalizing the distribution of a limited number of positions among the castes and communities into which a society is divided. In India it is being increasingly argued that education and employment, or the benefits thereof, should be more equitably distributed between the various castes and communities through direct intervention by the state. That may be a good thing in itself, but it will not be the same thing as equality of opportunity in the accepted meaning of the phrase. Such intervention will strengthen, if not the state, then at least the kinds of collective identity which the makers of modern India had thought should be dissolved in the interest of creating equality between individuals.

[62] *Towards Equality*, p. 107.

[63] It is noteworthy that the Committee on the Status of Women recommended against quotas for women, although there were dissenting notes against the recommendation.

Index